JUST LET HER
DANCE

FROM THE SOUTH SIDE TO BROADWAY

ONE GIRL'S JOURNEY INTO THE WORLD OF DANCE

PAULA LELAND

Published by Victorious You Press™

Printed in the United States of America

ISBN: 978-1-952756-54-2

DEDICATION

For My Family

CONTENTS

ACKNOWLEDGEMENTS

I would like to express special gratitude to my entire family for their nonstop love and encouragement. First, Mom and Dad, thank you for allowing me to grow and ultimately find my purpose. Not once did you criticize or doubt your baby girl. I know you are smiling from heaven.

The best gift my parents ever gave me was that of siblings: Deb, Dara, and James. You have all contributed in your own special way by simply supporting me since the very beginning. I love you all to the moon. My beloved, your love and support extend beyond the simplicity of words. Thank you for keeping the fire lit.

My dance teachers, Adrienne, and Ms. Johnson, thank you for pushing me creatively.

Mr. Grovic, my sixth-grade teacher, who saw something special in this little girl from the south side. Every child deserves a teacher like you.

Hearts of love are being sent to my dear friends for believing in me, sometimes more than I believed in myself.

Lovingly yours,

Paula Leland

THE DISCOVERY

Chapter I – The Block

"Ma, I want you to go on my field trip with me," I can recall saying. Remember that age when you still wanted to be around your parents? You also didn't mind your friends being around them either. Ma didn't go on many school outings with us; Daddy went on even fewer, but this one, I remember vividly. Imagine being in the fourth grade, maybe around age nine, sitting in the most extravagant and lavish auditorium in the city of Chicago. It's in the middle of one of our harshest winters, and you're waiting for the enchanting production to take centerstage. My classmates and I sink into the deep plush seats of the Arie Crown Theater, mesmerized by the whimsical stage décor of the performance. The backdrop is reminiscent of a scene from Willy Wonka and the Chocolate Factory, like sugar plum treats laced with snow-clouds of icing, a delectable child-like dream.

During that magical time of the year, when nearing the holidays, my school took all of us eager-beaver children to see The Nutcracker Ballet. I can't ever recall my teacher explaining the contextual narrative of the little blond girl dancing around with the toy soldier. Yet, it didn't block my appreciation of what I was about to see. I didn't fully grasp the storyline, but that didn't matter. I was ever so excited to be among the architecture and skyscrapers. The Arie Crown Theater was within proximity of downtown, and we would be able to get a glimpse of the beautiful Chicago skyline. Honestly, this wasn't the first time I've seen this production. In fact, this was probably my third. It was almost a ritual that we could depend on, at least one school outing every holiday season. But this excursion sparked something altogether different. The mood was *electric.*

Finally, convincing my mother to go, made this trip even more energetic. Having her tag along, made this particular performance of the Nutcracker most fascinating. The safety and security her presence provided left me with a feeling of comfort, protection, and confidence. I knew mid-way into the performance, something magical and supernatural had begun to stir in my little fourth-grade spirit. Whatever this feeling was, it was burning to be released. The majestic curtains cascaded into a black hole in the ceiling. The stage illuminated when the house lights darkened, causing our giddy little hands to roar with excited applause.

My neighborhood was the by-product of the great white flight. There was one white family left when we moved on the block, two elderly sisters, and everyone took care of them. Upwardly mobile African Americans were now filling up spaces in the neighborhood schools, Parent Teacher Associations, churches, local politics, parks, and libraries.

My childhood was incredible! It was safe and fun, and most of all, it consisted of neighborly *Love*. It was during a time when everyone looked out for each other's families, regardless if they birthed you or not. We had a very active block club, and while I didn't realize it at the time, I learned the temperament to our safety rested on the active involvement of the adults leading the community. Luckily for us, our parents knew this, and they stayed available, present, and engaged. More importantly, they taught their children to do the same.

The early years were extraordinary! There were four of us. I was the third of four siblings. My brother, Bub, was the youngest, and I had two older sisters, Denice and Darice. My parents worked hard, really hard, to provide for us. As a child, I honestly thought we were wealthy. We weren't. It was just my parents owned property and instilled in us the importance of hard work. When a tenant moved out, Daddy made us clean the empty spaces to prepare them for the next family. My sisters and I hated this part, but we dared not say it aloud. While I didn't recognize it then, these buildings provided shelter, clothing, food, girl scouts, cheerleading, choir, dance lessons, ushering, roller skates, pool table, ping-pong, and many other time-fillers for restless preteens.

As we grew into teen years, my sister, Darice, and I quickly learned how to get out of this menacing work. We're eighteen months apart and did pretty much everything together. I basically followed her around. We soon discovered, if we agitated daddy long enough, we would piss him off, and he would eventually shoo and hiss us away from his presence. My sister and I hated the gruesome toiling work of rehabbing the apartments. Daddy would fuss and complain of our goofy and silliness. What did he expect from two pubescent preteens? We were not professional painters, and besides, we'd rather be outside jumping double-dutch.

"Put the rollers down. I'll do it my damn self!" Daddy shouted. We pretended to sulk until we were out of his sight and then headed straight outside to play with our friends. Daddy pretended to be upset, but we knew it only lasted about five minutes. No, seriously, Daddy never stayed angry with us for very long. I'm sure it was because naturally, we were daddy's girls. As a matter of fact, we never took his threats seriously either. We had him wrapped around our little finger. I know, I know we were the worst. "Y'all on punishment for a week. No playing outside, and I mean that!" Daddy would firmly say as he reprimanded us, drastically reducing our exposure to sunlight. However, as soon as he would leave the house, we would wait maybe thirty minutes, and back outside we would go to soak up some Vitamin D.

When we saw Daddy's car return, we didn't even pretend to run back into the house because we were busted anyway. Daddy would walk right past us and not pay us any mind, perhaps forgetting or either not caring that minutes ago he had just placed us on punishment. Our friends had no idea that we were just grounded an hour earlier. Besides, they would woo our father with their social grace and charm. "Hello, Mr. Kuykendal." "Good afternoon, Mr. Kuykendal. Beautiful day isn't it, Sir?" He always spoke warmly to our friends, and they thought he was the nicest, dopest dad on the planet; and most of the time, he actually was. Daddy seldom questioned his two-middle-troublesome kids. Instead, he'd give us that look, and instead of being overcome with fear, mostly, we would instantly bust up laughing, knowing all was forgiven in the Kuykendal concubine. "Yea, our Dad was the best!"

Meanwhile, the memories of the dancers effortlessly twirling on their toes filled my head. They glided as beautiful swans. I was entranced with their movement, the colors, and the music. I took it all in. I fell most in love with the costumes and the ballerinas dancing on their toes, which I later learned, was called en pointe. I was captivated. I tapped my mother, leaned in, and said, "I'm going to dance on that stage one day." Ma quickly hushed me and nodded in agreement as if saying, *"Shhhhh...no talking in the theater, baby girl."* I didn't know how, and I didn't know when; all I knew was I had just been exposed to something so artistically and wonderfully beautiful. What I witnessed, lit a fire in the belly of my soul. This inspired me to discover, explore, and learn as much as I could about the mesmerizing world of *dance*.

The very next day after school, I rushed home and grabbed our encyclopedia collection. Not knowing where to begin, I grabbed the hefty "D" volume and spelled the word dance aloud. This was my start. D.A.N.C.E. I appreciated the encyclopedias and their glossy pictures. This was *Love*. I could search for a topic and get lost for hours on end. It was our dated version of Google. I skimmed the pictures looking for anything remotely similar to what was observed on stage in the Nutcracker Ballet. *"Ah, I found it; here it is,"* I said to myself—dancers performing ballet that originated during the Italian Renaissance. I slid the "D" back into its nook and reached for the "B." I took a seat at the dining room table and searched *B-A-L-L-E-T*. I got it. First, I explored the visuals. There were so many stunning pictures. I studied each one intently. The positions of the feet, the carriage of the arms, the head tilts, the leg extensions, every illustration became my motion in poetry. Next, I memorized each term, each expression, over and over again. The book of *B* had become my new-found best friend.

Margie was really my best friend growing up on the block. She was beautiful, sassy, funny, and had a fine older brother named Tariq, who just happened to be the nicest, coolest big brother on the planet. He was into Roger Nelson, aka Prince. No, let me retract that. That was an understatement. He worshipped Prince, and on a few lucky occasions, we got to hear a jam session, listening to some of his albums. Her brother could defend a Roger Nelson dissertation if he wanted to. Even though we were only twelve years old, listening to Prince made us feel so mature.

However, on days when Margie thought we were giving Tariq too much attention or when she was being the needy middle child, you could hear her yelling for her mom, Tricey, to intervene. "Ma! Tariq is stealing my friends! Tell him to stop!"

Depending on the particular day of the week and the number of adult beverages consumed, sometimes Tricey would scream back, "Tee, leave your sister's friends alone!" or sometimes we'd get "Margie! Don't you start! He. Is. Not. Stealing Your Friends!"

Either way, Tariq never retorted with a slick remark back. Her antics never fazed him, making him look even more mature and made Margie look like the bratty little kid sister. Tariq continued being the nicest, finest, and of course, coolest big brother.

Darice and I never understood Margie's territorial stance, and whenever her bratty selfish behavior was really annoying, we would pretend we had to go home. We chalked it up to the middle-child syndrome. Laughing and mocking her on our way home, I'd say, pretending to cry with all the extra dramatics, "Ma, T is stealing my friends."

Darice would then say, "Margie, you bet' NOT start!"

The two of us would holler with laughter all the way home. Despite Margie's juvenile ways, we had a lot of fun together. The next day I met up with her outside on the block. When there isn't much to do, or we've gotten tired of playing the same games, sometimes we'd just walk around, anything to prevent being couped up in the house. I loved this about Margie; we would make our own fun. This was one of those days where we just walked and talked about everything under the sun.

"Hey, I think I want to learn how to dance,"

"Girl, you already know how to dance," and she broke out doing the running man.

"No, not like that," I laughed, "but like they dance on the stage, the ballet. I've been thinking about this since seeing The Nutcracker."

"I hated The Nutcracker! Why do they take us to see that every single year! It's STUPID."

"Well, I think the costumes are beautiful. Don't you?"

"Nope."

I pretended to hold my imaginary skirt, spinning in a complete circle before jumping out the way of a speeding bike.

Margie shouted, "Stupid ass! Watch where you're riding!" The rebellious teen didn't slow down or stop. He threw up his middle finger at us and kept racing his yellow and green Schwinn down the street. We laughed hysterically and continued walking. Margie said, "I took ballet classes before and hated it. I was about four years old, and you know my Aunt Yvette who lives in Milwaukee?"

"Yeah, Kenny's mother, right?"

"Yeah, she got Ma to put me in dance. I took classes for two weeks and cried every single time. Told Ma, I didn't wanna go back."

"You didn't like it?"

"Nope! Not at all. Besides, I was four, remember?"

"Would you be interested in taking ballet now, perhaps?"

"The same way I'd be interested in walking over hot coals. Nope, still not interested. Aunt Yvette used to be a dancer, and she traveled all over the world."

"Really?" I was growing more intrigued. I never knew of anyone who was a professional dancer. I said, "Aunt Yvette definitely reminds me of a dancer."

Aunt Yvette was indeed pretty, and it wasn't hard imagining her as a dancer in her younger years.

"Did Kenny learn how to dance from her?"

"Girl, I don't know. As long as I can remember, he always knew how to dance, even when he was a baby."

Every fall, our neighborhood block club would sponsor a talent show. Margie's cousin, Kenny, would come from Wisconsin to perform his Michael Jackson routine. He was *that* good. Imagine ten to twelve impulsive preteen girls screaming hysterically at his performance like he was the real Michael Jackson. "Shake your body down to the ground," I did my best MJ impersonation. Kenny was fourteen with an already established fan club on the south side of Chicago.

First position, heels touch, feet turn out, almost duck-like. Hmmm, second position, heels are now apart, toes facing at an angle. There was also a third, a fourth, and a fifth position, but why would anyone want to contort their feet like that? The fifth position looked painful and almost impossible to maneuver. I hopped out of my dining room chair and forced my feet crisscrossed to overlap. I looked back at the glossy picture and down at my failed attempt. I desperately tried to straighten my legs without tumbling over and falling. Crash! I fell front-forward into the dining room table.

"Patrice!" Ma yelled.

"I'm ok," I jumped up to reassure her. The picturesque dancers with their sleek bun and solemn faces stood there as if they were mocking me from the pages of the encyclopedia. I stared back, intent on achieving mastery of the feet positions.

Every waking opportunity, I studied their frame, the lines from each photograph, the head tilt, every minor detail. I was in love with the pictures, but the words began to call me too. I then began examining the text. This book of B was my new life now. Read, study, imitate, repeat. Read, study, imitate, repeat. First position, "Ma, look, this is the first position of the feet," I told her.

Whenever Ma was called, she would instantly search for which child's voice was summoning for her attention. "Nice," Mama replied without flinching and went back to multitasking of cooking and talking to her girlfriend on the phone.

Ballet is a type of dance that originated during the Italian Renaissance in the fifteenth century. I began to study the writing, the words, fully submerging myself into this European culture of influence. I continued my study. I kept reading but often found myself rehearsing the position of the feet until I was able to demonstrate each one without looking in the book. Arms came next, and I added each pose to coincide correctly with the feet. I wanted to emulate each motion and pose. First position, heels together, arms cupped slightly below waist level. Second position, hold the arms out wide to match the feet. Every day after school, read, study, imitate, and repeat. Read, study, imitate, and repeat until I no longer needed to look at the pictures in the book of B. My audience of one, was my Ma, who often provided validation of my novice dance mastery.

Later, I saw Margie outside and yelled, "Ask your Aunt Yvette if she knows where I can take ballet?"

"Ok, she lives for stuff like that. I'll let you know what she says."

"Thanks." I continued to search for any books I could find on dance. At school, during library time, I picked up a book on Maria Tallchief. She was a Native American, part of the Osage Tribe. She was a principal ballerina with the New York City Ballet. She also married famed choreographer, George Balanchine. He was the artistic director of the New York City Ballet. In her book, she spoke of being Native American and the importance of her cultural heritage. I didn't fully understand why, but her enriching legacy resonated with me. She referred to herself as an American Indian Princess, and she definitely looked like a princess in her costumes and tiara. That appealed to me because she was proud of her legacy. Her picture book was enthralling to me as a little girl, and I studied it constantly. As a matter of fact, some of the pictures looked eerily similar to photos I've seen of my paternal great-great-grandmother. Maria Tallchief danced in my head and heart, and I continued to be inspired by her journey, her training, and her passion for ballet.

THE DISCOVERY

Chapter II – Sammy Dyer

The next day, Margie called me. "Aunt Yvette said to call her. She has some information to give you about dancing schools." I wrote her number down and hung up, agreeing to walk to the candy store later. I looked at the piece of paper that read Sammy Dyer School of the Theater. I tucked it under my pillow and headed out the door. I met Margie in front of her house. Puzzled, I asked about Sammy Dyer School of the Theater.

"That's where she used to dance...at Sammy Dyer in Chicago," Margie said.

"Oh, ok," I didn't have the slightest idea what she was referring to.

"Aunt Yvette was a Dyerette."

"What's a Dyerette?"

"Just call her; she'll tell you everything you want to know. Remember, she lives for that kind of stuff. She will talk your ear off, but Ma would always say, don't let her." Inside, I was bursting with joy because I was getting closer to my dream of taking dance classes.

When I came back home, I asked Ma if I could take dance classes.

"What kind of class?"

"Ballet, or something, I don't really know yet."

"Where would you go?"

"I'm not sure yet, but I'm looking. Margie's Aunt Yvette used to dance, and she said I could call her to find out about some places."

Ma looked at me but wouldn't commit. Instead, she said, "Ok, get the information, and your dad and I will consider it." That was enough for me to hear. I knew I could always count on their support.

"Hello, may I speak to Ms. Yvette? This is Patrice, Margie's friend."

"This is Yvette."

"Margie said it was ok to call you to find out the names of some dancing

schools."

"Sure, what kind of dance do you want to do?"

"Ballet, I think." My words sounded more of a question instead of a statement.

"Have you ever taken ballet or dance lessons before?"

"Ughh, no, I haven't." She instructed me to find something to write with.

"Ok, I'm ready."

"I want you to write the number to Sammy Dyer School of Theater. I used to

dance there. It's how I got my start. I became one of the Dyerettes."

"Margie, mentioned you traveled all over the world dancing, and what's a Dyerette?"

"Yes, the Dyerettes were the professional dance company of the studio. We

were named after the owner and director, Mr. Sammy Dyer himself. We were the first all-female-black professional dance group who performed with Duke Ellington and Sarah Vaughn, just some of the big names who hired beautiful, black, talented dancers back then. The history and legacy are so important, which is why I love sharing this information with any young person who will listen. We are so much more than what the media depicts on TV. There are more performing creative opportunities today for African Americans than when I was your age. Sammy Dyer saw something special in my technique, and he wanted to develop it even further. This is why he started his dancing school. So young people just like yourself could have access to top-notch, affordable training on the south side of Chicago." Aunt Yvette relished in sharing her story. "Give them a call at 312.233.1333 and tell them I referred you."

I felt transported in time and was grateful for the invaluable history lesson. "Thank you, Ms. Yvette. I will."

"And you can call me, Aunt Yvette." I hung up and dialed the number.

A pleasant voice answered. "Sammy Dyer, may I help you?"

"Uh, I'm calling to get information on your dance classes."

"Well, sweetie, give me your address. I'll send you our brochure. Then you can see which class is of interest to you. Also, if you like, you can take a free class. How old are you?"

"Eleven." She sounded friendly. I could actually *feel* her smiling through the phone.

"Excellent! I think our ballet, tap, jazz combination will be perfect for you.

Have your parents register you for a free class on Saturday at 10:00 am. We're located at 2400 S. Michigan. I think you are going to love it." I wrote down every single word.

"Thank you. I'm going to tell my mom. I slammed down the phone and rushed from my parent's room to the kitchen.

"Ma, I found a place. Can I take dance on Saturday? She said I could try it out, but you or daddy gotta bring me to register for ballet, tap, and jazz. It's called Sammy Dyer School of Theater, and Aunt Yvette was a famous Dyerette there." With my last breath, I belted, "Please! Can I go?"

"Whoa, slow down, baby girl." I didn't realize how fast I must have been talking.

"Now, start all over again, and who is this SHE?" Mom gave me a puzzling look with one eyebrow raised that said, *"Chile, what have you signed up for now?* She just shook her head in disbelief.

Ma called Sammy Dyer back and got all the details— including the clothes, shoes, type of dance class, cost, schedules, and address. The lady told her I could take a tap and ballet class because tap alternates weekly with jazz, but all dancers are required to take ballet without exception. She said not to worry about the tap shoes just yet, they would loan me a pair for the class, but I needed to come with my own ballet slippers.

Ma had Denice, my oldest sister, pick up my ballet slippers. Denice was six years older and thought she was the boss. And when Ma wasn't home, she was left in charge. I was quick to remind her that she was not my momma, which caused us to be polar opposites. Denice worked part-time at Sears, and Ma gave her my list of items to get. Lucky for me, they had everything I needed for class. Tired from school and work, Denice walked in and threw my bag on the table.

"Here you go." She sounded annoyed. "The man said to let him know if the shoes fit cuz they run small. He suggested getting one size larger."

I was half-listening to her rant. I ripped the package open and slipped them on.

Ma asked, "How do they fit? Come here." She treated them like they were school shoes, pinching my toes. "I can feel your toes at the tip." She looked at her oldest child and asked, "Is that how they're supposed to fit?" My sister shrugged her shoulders, went to her room, and closed the door.

"Yes! They fit!" I answered for her. I really didn't know how they were *supposed* to fit. I just knew I was one step closer to being in dance class. I was completely awash with emotion. I couldn't freaking believe it. I actually had on *"real ballet slippers."* This had to be a dream. Ma was the best!

Saturday morning came, and I was up bright and early. Mom instructed me to put my black leotard and white tights under my clothes. It was a fall day with my Virgo birthday quickly approaching in September. I didn't know what to expect from class. Sure, I studied the pictures forever and a day, but this was different. I was going to my first dance class. This was surreal. I pictured myself in the encyclopedia having all the arm and feet positions memorized correctly.

Darice decided to tag along to Sammy Dyer. Generally, we fight for the front seat, like Every. Single. Time. I mean, what is it about the front seat that's so appealing? My sister and I almost started World War III by calling dibs on the front seat. However, this day was unique and entirely different. I didn't do my usual sprint to the car or try to shove her hand from the grip of the door handle. We didn't have our normal cantankerous fit or fistfight about sitting in the back row. This time was altogether distinctive. I was unusually quiet. My mind was preoccupied with anxious thoughts. The nerves were taking hold of my angst. What if my dancing looked appalling, and I'm unable to keep up, and I'm embarrassed? What if I'm mocked, and people laugh at me? Ma would be forgiving because she's my mom, and she truly loves me unconditionally. However, my sister, that's another conversation because she wouldn't let me live it down. I can see her rushing into the house just to happily announce the travesty that just took place. Then to make matters worse, she exaggerates and lies. It would play out like this,

"Hey, y'all! Guess what P did at the dancing school?" I would then pretend to be unbothered as the humiliation begins. *"She was awful, terrible, dreadful. As the dancers went right, guess which direction P went? Yup...you got it. LEFT!"* Everyone would bowl over from hysterics, laughing

uncontrollably. I started to second guess myself. Maybe this is a bad idea altogether. I was inside of my head.

Ma looked back and asked, "You ready?"

"Uh-huh," I managed to say.

Darice turned to look at me and affirmed, "Don't embarrass the Kuykendal's name either because you would not live it down, and I'll make sure of that."

"Shut up." I rolled my eyes at her.

My heart was thumping. My mind was racing. I had to get out of my own way. That's the thing about fear. It can create all types of nuisances. Nuisances that don't even exist that could literally paralyze your confidence and shrink your self-esteem to the size of a jellybean. We got out of the car, and I slammed the door.

Darice asked, "Aren't you leaving your dance bag, stupid?" She shook her head in disbelief.

"Oh, yeah." I quickly opened the door to grab it. Ma gave a slight grin and wink to Darice. As if to say, *go easy on her.* She knew her baby girl was uncomfortably nervous.

On the outside, the building was discreet and unobtrusive with tan bricks and one large window. The tint on the window was dark. It allowed people to see outside but not inside. And there it was, the historic name right above the awning in bold black letters, *Sammy Dyer School of Theater.* While waiting to be buzzed in, I casually looked at the surroundings on Michigan Avenue. There weren't many businesses, except a Burger King across the street and the notable Chicago Defender newspaper on the adjacent corner. Other than that, a few office spaces littered an otherwise desolate block.

Upon entering the grand building, the office manager handed Ma papers for registration. She spoke dignified and regal, asking, "Are they both here to dance?" Darice quickly belted, "Noooooo way!" Ma immediately jolted her one of those *"Don't you dare start—we out in public looks."* I had to admit, it was pretty funny, which caused my nerves to relax a little. In addition to being regulated as the sibling chief bully, sister number two always had a grand way of making me laugh at the right time.

The receptionist's name was Miss Williams. She, too, had been a Dyerette Dancer back in the day. I recognized her photo on one of the famed walls in the halls. It was nostalgic. Pictures of Sammy Davis Jr. and other celebrities greeted you as you entered. I didn't recognize everyone, but Ma explained who they were.

I pointed and said, "That's Aunt Yvette, Margie and Tariq's aunt."

"Which one?"

"The third from the end." I directed Darice to a picture labeled, "The Dyerettes!" They posed stunningly in black fishnets and sequined tuxedo jackets. There were six in the picture, and they were all gorgeous. I asked, "Miss Williams, is that you?"

She proudly replied, "Why, yes." She still had the body of a dancer and the face of a model. Ms. Williams politely said, "You have ten minutes to change before class begins."

I went to the changing area and quickly returned with my street clothes packed in my bag. I handed it to my Ma. I was trembling.

Miss Williams noticed my goose bumps and whispered to me, "Go on, it's going to be fine." She opened the door to the ballet studio and gave me a gentle push inside. Ma and Darice waited patiently while I took ballet and tap. The school's policy mandated you must participate in all classes. I have to admit, I wasn't the least bit motivated to learn how to tap dance, but Sammy Dyer required all students to follow a very regimented class schedule. Ballet provided our foundation. It was considered the holy grail of dance, so we took it every week, alternating with tap and jazz. Miss Williams explained to Ma, "Mr. Dyer wanted his dancers to be well-rounded and to develop a solid work ethic." In other words, you follow our program, or you don't. All classes came as a package deal.

Miss Johnson, the ballet mistress, was already doing demi plies in front of the mirror. I knew it was a plie because I studied the word a thousand times. Plie to bend using the knees. Demi plie: Demi (French) meaning small, a small or slight bend of the knees. Grande plie: Grande

(French) meaning large, a deep bend of the knees. I literally ate the book of B encyclopedia for breakfast, lunch, and dinner.

Miss Johnson softly asked, "Dear, what's your name?"

"Patrice," I sputtered.

"Have a seat in the middle of the floor. The others will be here momentarily."

There was one other girl already in class. She looked older, like a teenager. I could tell she was a regular because she was stretching and warming up her body as if she was getting ready for the Olympics. I tried not to look intimidated, but she was good. I mean really good. I thought, *"If she's in my class, Boy, I have a long way to go."* I studied her closely. She was so centered on her study; I don't think she knew I was in the room. Her level of concentration was awe-inspiring. I noticed what I thought was a birthmark on the side of her neck as she completed shoulder isolations. It stood out because it was shaped like the letter V. I decided to channel her energy and use it for inspiration and motivation. She reminded me of one of the ballerinas from the book.

Miss Johnson didn't seem mean. She appeared very stoic. She definitely didn't smile or go out of her way to be congenial. She wore her hair slicked back in a bun, the same way I had seen in the pictures hundreds of times. I thought, *"Maybe hair buns are a requirement of ballet?"* She spoke softly but firm. I could tell by her stance; she

25

took ballet very seriously and required her students to do the same. Tall and regal looking, she still had the body of a dancer. She looked much older in the face than the receptionist, Miss Williams. I wondered if she, too, had been a Dyerette? I didn't recall seeing her picture on the wall. I fantasized, maybe she danced with Maria Tallchief.

As the others started to enter class, the teenage student who was stretching earlier quickly left the studio. Miss Johnson explained she was one of her advanced students and directed everyone to the ballet bar. I looked at the others and just followed along. I thought, maybe one day, I'll be as good as that teenager.

Miss Johnson stood in the center and demonstrated arm movement with first position plies. She asked, "Any questions?" No one said a word. It was eerily quiet, as if no one was even breathing. I noticed the consternation tone of the room. At that moment, I fully understood the seriousness and significance of learning ballet techniques. Her faceless expression read, *"This is why ballet class is a must every single week. It is the most respected class when developing and training young dancers."*

I'll never forget my very first dance teacher, Miss Johnson. She demanded and expected nothing short of giving 110% of yourself, week after week. She was determined to transform us into dancers. One little brown face at a time. She could care less if this was your first day or your fifth day of class. She contorted and twisted our little bodies until we got it right. I can vividly see Miss Johnson moving the needle on the phonograph to play Chopin for class, rhythmically counting, "Five, six, seven, eight," in what would become my very first experience in ballet class.

My parents called me into their bedroom and asked if I really wanted to take dance class. In our household, you are summoned to the bedroom when it's a serious topic of discussion. My parents were good cop and bad cop. Daddy never played the bad cop role. It must have been sealed in their marriage contract. Daddy was associated with everything fun, while Ma was left with the role of disciplinarian and enforcer.

Dad spoke first, "If we're gonna pay for classes, then you have to keep your grades up."

"Ok, I will," I said excitedly. Grades were hardly discussed in our household. It's not like they weren't important; it was just an unspoken expectation. Teachers loved the Kuykendal children. We were well-behaved, active, and smart. So, daddy speaking about grades was a no-brainer.

Next was the enforcer's turn, "Now, your daddy and I are not going to be able to take you every Saturday."

"Uhhh, how would I get there?" I was slightly confused.

"So, if you really want to take dance, we will teach you how to catch the bus on the days when we won't be available to pick you up." My eyebrows crinkled. I didn't care.

"Ok."

Good cop chimed in, "We'll get your sister to ride with you."

"Ok." I left their room dancing on cloud nine. Taking the bus didn't bother me one bit. I was excited and ready to discover this new journey.

THE DEVELOPMENT

Chapter III – Popular Coconuts

I turned my shared bedroom dresser into a makeshift studio to practice my ballet at home. Stretching my leg horizontally on my bed helped me with my splits. My newfound flexibility aided me in cheerleading too. My sister and I commanded the cheerleading squad. We participated and won most cheer competitions for our school. Darice was pretty and popular. I'm really being hyperbolic on the pretty part. You see, I was popular by default. I mean, you can't actually be a cheerleader and *not* be popular, right? And as the little sister to the captain of the team, I definitely scored free participation points. Or, as Keleila, my high school friend, would say, "You and Darice sure are 'Miss Popular Coconuts.'" I never quite understood that saying, but if you knew Keleila, she was dramatic and had a way with words. Now, don't get me wrong, I was in noooo way as popular as Darice, but I was content being in her shadow. Being in her background was safe, easy, and a role that I didn't mind playing.

In my elementary years, I was a little thing, small in size—so petite that I was comfortable being on the top of our cheer pyramids and thrown in the air for jumps and catches. I led the cheer line because we would line up according to height, and the shortest was always the first in line. I grew accustomed to standing on shoulders in our cheer formations and being the guinea pig when it was time to try out new tosses and cheer throws. I'd be remiss if I failed to mention the neglected catches and falls too.

Most people find it hard to believe that I was once petite, considering I grew to a whopping five feet ten inches. I attribute the growth spurt to seventh and eighth grade, where I shot up a whole four inches in one summer. Becoming taller garnered me a new nickname, "Too Tall Jones." Not only did my height shoot up, but my shoe size grew too. This led to further teasing. My feet kept growing to a size eleven while still in high school.

Darice began tormenting me because, according to her, shoes would no longer fit, and I had to opt to wear boots. I mean, when you think of it, it's quite a lame joke. But that didn't stop her or her friend, Gwen, from trying to roast me every chance they could. I took it all in jest, as only a little sister can. My comebacks failed miserably, but it didn't stop me from trying. With two against one, it was always a losing battle on my end. It neither deterred nor prevented me from constantly being around both of them. Guess I was a glutton for punishment. We were together so much that people thought the three of us were sisters.

Let me expound on the popularity of Darice. She wasn't just popular; she was good at practically everything—her school grades, cheerleading, majorette, and roller skating. You name it, she commanded it. Once, Darice was up for a double promotion in school, but my parents said no. Can you believe that? The teachers thought she was so smart that they recommended she skip sixth grade and go from fifth straight to seventh grade. Ma and Daddy refused, though. I wonder why? Behind closed doors, they probably knew she was basic smart, but not "*smart- smart.*" Her intellect was effortless, and getting good grades came easy. At her eighth-grade graduation, she was awarded the American Legion medal. It stood for excellence with an amazing regard for potential of academic success. As I said, she excelled in pretty much everything. Me, not so much. I had to actually put in the work.

School teachers enjoyed having the Kuykendal children in their class, but when it came to Darice, the teachers revered her. No, seriously, they ADORED every ounce of her DNA. Case in point, one day, Ma kept her home from school because she was sick. Do you know one of her teachers actually came to my class asking to see me? "Ms. Sharon, may I see Patrice?" I'm sure she probably didn't say my name, more like the Kuykendal girl.

31

"Patrice, Ms. West would like to see you."

Looking quite bewildered, I got up and headed for the door. In school, I was as quiet as a church mouse. I knew her teacher, Ms. West, though. In fact, everyone knew her teacher. She was flamboyant with the way she wore her hair, clothes, and makeup. Even the car she drove was a flashy convertible white Mercedes. She was that fun teacher who made the dentist money by illegally selling candy from her desk drawer, that is until the principal found out and shut her down. She was mad cool, and you knew the unpopular teachers probably tricked on her. No wonder Darice wanted to be just like her. She was everyone's favorite. I stepped into the hall.

Ms. West spoke, "I know Darice's not feeling well today. I spoke to your mother. So, I'm sending home a tray of butter cookies with you. I'll bring them at the end of the day."

"Uh-ok." I went back to my seat.

My friend whispered, "What did she want?"

Baffled, I looked at her and said, "She's sending me home with a tray of butter cookies."

In slow motion replay, my friend's mouth dropped and said, "Nooooo way."

School dismissal is at 2:30 pm, but at exactly 2:25pm, Ms. West handed me a tray of twenty-four butter cookies securely wrapped in plastic on a lunchroom tray. You see my point?

Darice perked up and instantly felt better after seeing me walk in the house with two dozen cookies from her idol. She begged Ma to let her go outside and disturbingly, Ma acquiesced. Darice claimed she was feeling better and just like that she was allowed outdoors. I fumed with jealousy because that would have never happened to me. The stoic rule would have read, "Patrice, no school, no outside."

"Why does Darice get to go outside? She didn't even go to school today?" I questioned.

"Don't worry about me." She said rather curtly and nastily. Raising up her middle finger while licking out her tongue out of Ma's view.

"Ma, she cussing," I said.

Cutting her eyes in my direction, she said "Am not! Stupid, if I was cussing, Ma would hear me. It's not like her ears don't work." She sucked her teeth.

Pleading, Ma said, "Don't y'all start. Go outside and play off some of that energy."

The back-and-forth banter between me and Darice was a constant nonstop. It drove Ma crazy that we fought a lot.

Although she got on my reserve nerves, I loved having a permanent playmate. I was never without someone to play with. Sure, we stayed at each other's throats but Darice really was my best friend and secretly, I wanted to be just like her.

"Hey, how do you twirl the star with your left hand?" I asked Darice admiring her gifted twirling versality.

"Like this." She paraded her skills with the right hand then simply switched to her left without dropping the baton or knocking it into her elbow.

I tried again. "Ouch!!" The metal end cascaded into my bone.

"Look!" She was showing off, twirled the baton and threw it in the air while doing a 360 turn, and caught it all in one swoop. She was bad! "So!" She twirled the metal bar slower to teach me. "Do it this way." She twirled even slower. I tried again. "Better." Then, in hand-over-hand motion, she air-marked the pattern to help me gesture the twirl correctly.

I allowed her to guide my fingers and wrist until I finally perfected the move.

"That's it! You got it, grasshopper!"

"I got it! I got it!" An effusive smile warmed my heart as I continued to twirl. Her remarks reminisced of a pleased older sister. She always helped me when I needed her to and pulled back when it was time for me to fly. Like I said, she was great at pretty much everything.

I started Sammy Dyer officially in sixth grade. I was in Mr. Grovic's classroom. He was probably the fifth most popular teacher at my school. He rode a motorcycle to work, and every day at dismissal, the kids would freeze like statues watching him pass by, gallantly waving to him. We all thought it was the coolest, yet, strangest thing to witness. Your teacher is *actually* on a motorcycle.

My Saturdays now consisted of 9:00 am ballet followed by 10:30 am Jazz. Jazz alternated with Tap at 10:30 am. They also made you squeeze in acrobats on rotating days. Dance class was my life now. I took my study very seriously. My parents drove me to dance on Saturday mornings for the first year. On many days, I was dropped off and picked up three hours later. Ballet was laborious and slow and quiet and methodical and controlled and soft and graceful and unlike anything I've ever done. I learned classical music of Tchaikovsky, Beethoven, and Chopin. My miniature world was expansively growing.

The discipline of the art was very exacting, and I practiced any and everywhere I could. Whether I was walking in the grocer aisle with my mom or walking home from school, I practiced. I remembered being restless waiting in line to enter the restroom at school, and out of nowhere, I did a sur le cou-de-pied (strike neck of the foot).

Mr. Grovic said, "Kuykendal, what's that thing you just did with your foot?" He was a military man, and he called us by our last name—another reason to love him.

"Uh, oh, I'm sorry," I replied. Without realizing that ballet was becoming ingrained in my psyche. I would daydream I was on stage in front of thousands of people.

Again, he said, "What's that thing you just did with your foot?"

"Sur le cou-de-pied, it's ballet."

"Oh wow! How long have you been in ballet?"

"I just started three months ago."

Mr. Grovic must have experienced a premonition of my future because he said, "Kuykendal, one day, you're going to perform on Broadway!"

At that time, I honestly didn't understand the magnitude of his declaration, nor did I know where this place called Broadway was actually located. All I knew was that it must be something special if my favorite teacher just manifested this into my life. I smiled and quickly regained my composure to remain still in the school hallway. For the rest of the day, I couldn't stop thinking about this place called Broadway.

THE DEVELOPMENT

Chapter IV – The Blizzard

I adored ballet, but we had a complicated relationship. It was unyielding and unforgiving towards mastering the technique. After three months of methodical growth, Miss Johnson instructed me to position myself, either at the front or at the end of the ballet barre. This directive was reflective of her confidence in my talent in being able to lead the barre instruction in class. My heart was beaming and expanded on the inside. The best dancers are often strategically placed at opposite ends of class, so regardless of which side you're working on, you're able to have a strong lead to follow. Those chosen to be in the front, generally have the best technique and can guide the other dancers by example.

As I became more acquainted with dance, my confidence grew, and I quickly learned that in order to gain the teacher's approval, hard work was required and expected. My dance continued to improve, and it showed in the strength of my technique. The timing was perfect as I began to catch the attention of the higher-ups at the studio as we prepared for our annual spring recital.

If you wanted to perform in the recital, attendance in every class was mandatory. The only excused absence accepted was either illness or some other unforeseen emergency. And by emergency, I mean you were in the hospital, unable to attend rehearsal. I fully understood the parameters and guidelines of the studio. We were now learning choreography for our upcoming performance, and if you missed class, then you also missed staging, blocking, and any notes given. This could cause you to fall terribly behind and slow down the entire production.

I was fully committed 110 percent, and nothing was going to hold my progress back—not even the brutal winters of the Chicago cold. Saturday morning began without much fanfare. I would get up, get dressed, pack my dance bag with my tights, leotard, and ballet shoes. I'm pretty orderly, and I like to keep all of my dance things in my special space inside my closet. We were required to wear hair off the face and dress in a black leotard, white tights, and pink or black slippers. The studio was very regimented and structured in protocols and procedures.

Since this was the Saturday that Mom worked, Dad was at home with the kids. I shouted from my room, "Who taking me to dance?"

Dad peaked his head in my room, "You're not going to dance today."

"Why not?"

"It's too cold! We're having a blizzard." I had to quickly collect my thoughts and tried to extend the conversation. "Daddy, I have to go! We're learning new choreography, and we're not allowed to miss class, not unless we are in the hospital. I have to GO!" Dad was uber cool and allowed nothing to faze him. I'm sure he was thinking, *""There's no conversation needed. You. Not. Going. And. That's. That!"* I needed him to really hear me and understand that I *had* to be at dance today. My whole life depended on it. Naturally, I did what any preteen would do when they don't get their way; I played my parents' power against each other. Don't get me wrong, I'm generally on *"Good-Cop/Team Dad,"* but Not today, no sir. I picked up the phone and called mom.

The operator spoke, "University of Chicago, how may I help you?"

"May I speak with Mary Kuykendal?" Ma's work voice was the warmest thing ever, so unlike her Momma's voice. She gently spoke in the receiver.

"This is Mary Kuykendal."

"Ma!" I yelled in her ear. "Daddy said I can't go to dance because it's too cold. I have to go. I just have to. I can take the bus; Margie will go with me. We're learning new choreography, and we're not allowed to miss it. Not for anything. It's for the show, Ma. I'll dress warm. I promise. Ms. Johnson said now is the time to get really serious. She said as a dancer, I must develop my talent, be committed and focus on the choreography. I paused to catch my breath.

Ma interjected, "Whoa, slow down."

"See, we're getting ready for the show, and I can't miss. Imma layer up, promise. Miss Johnson said we may get kicked out if we miss any rehearsals." The quickest way to get Ma to cave in was to call her at work. She didn't have time for my shenanigans and quickly solved whatever situation I was facing.

"Ok, tell your dad you can go, but you're sure Tricey is gonna let Margie go with you?"

"Yes, Tricey said she can go," I lied. I had to call and ask, and if needed, plead and hope Margie would be able to ride the bus with me on the coldest day of the year.

Ma's last words before she hung up were, "make sure you dress warm."

"I will." I got the answer I was seeking. I hung up and yelled from the other room, "Ma said I can go." I heard the door close, and daddy was out the door. Not sure if he heard me but as long as I had permission from one of the cops, I was good to go. Now, hopefully, Margie would also receive the same blessing.

"Margie, are you crazy? No, you cannot go!" Tricey yelled out as Margie sulked and closed the door.

If they knew I was going by myself, my parents would have forbidden me from going on that dreadful day. Instead, I said nothing and walked to the bus stop. It only took five steps on the iced pavement for the cold to snake up my back. I instantly felt the below subzero down my spine. It was brutally cold. The weather was unforgiving, vicious, and rancorous.

That's the thing about Chicago's winter. It truly is unlike any other region of frigid weather. This day was no different. I sloshed in the subterranean snow, which buried my knees. The fierce wind felt like someone slapped my face with a sheet of ice. My fingers were submerged deep into my pockets, neatly balled into a fist inside my gloves. My lack of energy forced me to drag my dance bag from behind. It was taking its toll on me. I tried to mask my fingers from the numbness of the cold. It didn't help. I felt all life exiting my extremities. Occasionally, I'd peek over my right shoulder just to make sure my dance bag was still being dragged from behind.

The northern wind off Lake Michigan was so strong that it pushed my small body to lead headfirst. I loved dance, but did I love it this much? I think I did. I started to second-guess my decision as the numbness spread to my toes. I read somewhere that I had five minutes left before my limbs were officially frostbitten. It was in a book. I prayed the bus would hurry. I glanced east and then west. No bus. I paced the street to keep the biting chill from settling in my bones. I scanned the street again for signs of the moving vehicle. Ughhh, still no bus. This went on for a solid five minutes and as if the heavenly gates opened, a bus finally appeared in view. The neon cherry sign flashed *"Out of order"* with every blink of an eyelash. "Damn!" I felt ultimately defeated.

Luckily, within a couple of minutes, another bus came to a slow halt. My fingers had a burning sensation to them, which I had read is the first sign of frostbite. I had no movement in my extremities. They were completely numb, followed by extreme itching. Which is the second sign of frostbite. The bus rolled to a complete stop and the doors butterflied open, allowing me access. The warmth of the heat jerked me onto the seventy-ninth street bus. The scene was so surreal; I wanted to cry. That's Chicago cold for you. It is wickedly inhumane and unrelenting. This short route to the L train station was blissful and dreamy. I savored the warmness of the heat for as long as I could before making my exit. I was back in the frigid-degree weather attempting to walk the remaining eight blocks to the studio on Cermak and Michigan avenue. What normally was a nippy ten-minute walk, took thirty long treacherous minutes. My mind was growing foggy, and there was ringing in my ears. I could not feel my toes or fingers at this point. I tried to block out the blizzard.

In true elementary fashion, I needed warmth and managed to stop by a candy store while climbing over mounds of packed snow. I waited for five minutes to get the blood circulating back in my body. By the time I arrived at the studio, my fingers and toes were definitely frostbitten. It was an extreme burning sensation, and my ears were ringing. Unbeknownst to me, the cold wind left tear tracks on my face with frozen snot that looked like icicles hanging from my eyelashes and nostrils. Yes, I was horribly late, but I didn't care because this Virgo was determined to get there.

I quickly unlayered and grabbed my dance bag. I reached inside for my ballet shoes. I grabbed one and placed it on my feet, wiggling my toes for any sign of life. They did not move. The tips of my toes and fingers felt prickly and once again, began to itch severely. I dug around for my other shoe. I moved my hand side to side, searching for a flat piece of leather to grab hold. Odd, I couldn't feel anything to grasp. I opened my bag, turned it inside out, and shook it violently upside down. My eyes peered into a colossal hole at the bottom of the bag. I shook it again. My moment of triumph quickly deflated. Irked and irate, I punched my fist on the floor and was quickly reminded of the frostbite. My hand swelled and became inflamed at the point of contact with the floor, and I started sobbing even harder. With immense anger, I yanked the bag and ripped the opening even further, causing the hole to widen. "I lost my damn shoe!" I yelled.

Sullenly, I entered class and looked around to see the near bare studio. Only two dancers showed up that day. And right in front of the class stood a piss-poor substitute of a teacher. I felt like imploding, thinking, *"I should have listened to my dad...ughhhhhh!"*

As time progressed, our rehearsals became more intense the closer we got to the date of the show. I was fixated on mastering the choreography. The artistic director, Shirley Bass, came into class and watched our rehearsed piece. She nodded her head as in deep thought, walking back and forth, covering the length of the studio. Ms. Bass started with Sammy Dyer as one of his lead dancers back in the 1960s. Striking and beautiful, she carried herself like royalty throughout the building, popping into every single class to offer blistering yet constructive critique. She was treated like royalty, more like a queen by the entire staff and revered by little girls like me who were in complete awe of her dance journey and her larger-than-life presence. Ms. Bass continued to carry Mr. Dyer's historic torch and legacy. She reminded everyone who entered the studio of the founding principles Of Sammy Dyer. Simply stated, they consisted of providing affordable top-tier dance techniques on the south side of Chicago.

Ms. Bass surveyed the room and abruptly stopped our choreography. She pointed to three dancers in the class. "You, you, and you step out and come to the center." Being one of the lucky ones, I quickly made my way to the middle of the floor. She said, "You three will be the dancing ponies in this piece." I had no clue what that meant, but I was thrilled and tried to humble my excitement! She motioned to Miss Johnson with directions, "Make sure they're fitted for the pony costumes."

Miss Johnson demurely replied, "Absolutely."

My talent was being noticed. To say I was excited was an understatement! I couldn't wait to share this news with my family.

Winter came and went as it does every season. Spring sprung with the forward setting of the clocks. Finally, a gentle breeze of warm weather graced the air. Hastily, my recital was quickly making its way closer and closer. I practiced every day and everywhere. In the grocery aisle with mom. At the dentist's office with dad. In my backyard and in whatever space I was able to hoard. I literally could not sit still. I'm surprised no one labeled me with a hyper-deficit disorder and tried to silence my artistic energy with prescriptive pills. I aggravated my siblings with my superfluous jumps, leaps, and high kicks, whizzing by whosever's head came within frame and inches from my foot. Luckily for me, my family tolerated my intolerable movement.

Dad drove me to my very first costume fitting. Being fussed over made me feel like a Star! The seamstress scheduled each class for a specific time for measurements. She was an older lady, and her workspace was consumed with bulks of fabric, tulle, lace, sequins, and shiny buttons to match. It reminded me of Hollywood glamour. Her glasses hung off the tip of her nose, and you had to repeat yourself at least twice in her good ear. She took the measuring tape from around her neck and whipped it around my frail waist. She yelled out some numbers, and her assistant quickly jotted down notes.

Hips, inseam, and length all followed. "Twenty, twenty-five, you got that?" She looked me up and down. "You're gonna be a tall one. Yep, I can tell." I didn't say a word and stood there doing as I was told. "Turn. Arms up. Other side." She looked up and asked, "Are you a pony?' You sure look like a pony," she whispered, then laughed.

I glanced over at my Dad, who was proudly standing by as if I was being fitted for my Oscar gown. I drifted into my Tony award acceptance speech for best performer. *"I couldn't have done this without the love and support from my family. They poured into my spirit the belief that I could dream big dreams and accomplish great things in..."* Startled, an agitated voice awoke me from my trance. This time with less patience, she asked again.

"Are. You. A. Pony?"

"Oh, yes, I'm a pony."

The first costume was for the ensemble number, a stiff satin tutu in a horrendous, Pepto Bismol-neon-pink color, bordered with white lace. It itched and scratched my skin something awful. The second one was a pure white romper with silver sequins and a matching choker. I guess it was supposed to make us look like ponies. The entire fitting took less than ten minutes, but this experience left me feeling celebrated and magnificent. I yearned for more!

Dress rehearsals were an altogether different story. One took place at the studio, which was a dry run-through of the entire show, and the other was what is called a tech run with costumes and live music. The almost three-hour production was divided into two parts. The first half focused on varying elements of theatrical dance, while the second half was dedicated to the continuum of a show musical. This component gave the show a more professional edge. This year's theme was "A Little Night Music." The dry run was held on a Saturday, generally three weeks prior to opening night, and it was an all-day event, 11:00 am–5:00 pm. The more intense dress rehearsal took place on a weeknight, which for me was also a laborious school night. It included costumes, union stagehands, and production assistants with the complete orchestra at the venue.

Dad often chauffeured me to and from dress rehearsals. He made sure I was on time for my 4:00 pm call and picked me up promptly at 9:00 pm dismissal. Quietly, I sensed his adoration and pride.

Ma's job was to make sure everyone had a ticket to my performance. Which often included my older cousin, Toni. She was my heart and old enough to be my aunt, but due to the law of genetics, she was my cousin. Toni supported me to the end of the earth, and it was a love I would forever treasure. Cousin Toni didn't own a car, so I wasn't sure if she knew how to drive or not. We always picked her up from her Hyde Park condominium and made sure she got back safely. With Cousin Toni in tow, we took two cars to the Arie Crown Theater to my performance.

My ridiculous call time was always three hours prior to curtains, which was a complete pain, considering at age twelve, I had no idea what we were supposed to do with all that extra time? Parents were not allowed to wait with their children because every stage mom would have been in full swing. They were instructed to drop their children off and "poof" be gone.

Backstage, we were able to hear the excitement and rustle of people finding their seats in the auditorium. Ma often shared stories of how proud dad was sitting in the audience waiting for me to dance on stage. She reminisced these moments when "Your dad would strike up a conversation with whoever listened.

"The tallest one, that's mine," he would boast.

"That one?"

Dad jubilantly answered, "Yea, the tall one."

My growth spurt was in full swing because I was getting taller and taller. I surpassed both of my sisters in height. Ma would tell me how Daddy just bragged on how he loved watching me perform. Listening to these stories made my heart bust with innocent joy!

The chatter from the audience made it hard to concentrate, and the roar of applause literally kept us on our toes. This only meant one thing. The show had finally begun, and the production assistants led us to our blocking for our first tap routine. We warmed up our ankles and mimed our time step. We froze as we waited for the curtains to lift. I kept remembering how immense the stage felt. The feeling was colossal and distinctive from the dress rehearsal. The entire stage was midnight, and the dazzling lights blocked everything. I tried to stop the anxiety from overpowering me. I focused on my shuffle ball chain and my pink satin costume. The venue overwhelmed me. It was massive and far-reaching, as I saw nothing but absolute darkness from seat to seat. This extended far into oblivion. *Oh, how I wish I could see the faces of my family,* but the obscurity prevented any of that.

The music began, and I dazzled with my tap technique and borrowed charm. I turned my smile on full charge and finished the tap number with a curtsy bow. In what seemed like an eternity, my fellow dancers and I flapped off-stage with our signature heel-toe-dig exit.

The theatrical imagery of the dressing rooms reminisces with Hollywood glamour like the pictures depicted in the old movies and television. Complete with makeup chairs and mirrors galore, this was a temporary makeshift space between costume changes. I quickly switched into my next number while meticulously placing my things back in my area for safekeeping.

"Hey, can you pass me that?"

I looked up, having one foot inside my tights. "What?"

She pointed at my things.

One of the dancers had misplaced her tights on my vanity. I hastily grabbed them and flicked them in her direction.

"Keep up with your freaking stuff! Can't you see this is the biggest night of my life?" was what I wanted to scream!

But instead, "No problem," rolled off my tongue with a slight eye roll.

Ms. Johnson walked in. "Lovely job. You are all simply wonderful," she beamed, smiling brightly, which was odd in itself because she hardly smiled the whole year of class. Maybe that smile had everything to do with not being required to teach in the summer and being free from explaining how your knees should go over your toes when you plie for the hundredth time.

"Hurry girls, you don't have much time before the second act. Where are my ponies? Girls, girls, now your costume is a variation. Come here, line up. Let me see you." We scuttled in line. "Beautiful, my darlings! Yes, perfect! Now prance like the best ponies in the world!" Ms. Johnson was really ecstatic. I liked this Miss Johnson much better than the dry version.

We were led to the seamstress with one final primp of nudging and pulling of our costume. The ballad, *"Send in the Clowns,"* was the dramatic score that opened the second act with a reprise. The orchestra's score of this iconic tune was led by percussions with a snare and bass drum intro. This marked the pony's spectacular entrance. With legs ever so high in the air, we frolicked and pounced until we made our way center stage. We danced like the life of a pony depended on it.

I basked in tonight's limelight. I was on fire from the thrill of actually being on stage. I was never going to forget the magic of this night. My family made their way backstage at the close of curtain call. Cousin Toni brought me flowers, and Daddy wanted to take the Kuykendal Crew to dinner. We didn't splurge often at restaurants, but tonight was a celebratory occasion.

Daddy said, "Baby Girl, where do you want to go? It's your night tonight."

"Sizzler."

"Sizzler, it is."

At dinner, we laughed and talked nonstop about how marvelous the entire show was. Daddy was still beaming with pride. He raised his glass to motion for a toast. "I think we have a superstar in the family."

Everyone laughed when Denice said, "Where?"

Jokes aside, I must have been good if my siblings complimented me.

Ma said, "Patrice, you know that's where we saw the Nutcracker with your class. Do you remember what you said?"

"Uh-huh, one day, I'm going to dance on that stage."

"Yes, you did. Yes, you did."

THE DEVELOPMENT

Chapter V — The Stranger

Bub, the only boy, is five years younger than me. Elated to finally have a son, Ma decided to make him a junior. Bub was into sports and played on the Blue Jays Little League baseball team. One of my dad's coworkers was the coach. We started calling him Bub because as he grew older, he hated the name Bubba. I think it stemmed from him being a little chubby baby with thick legs and fat club-looking feet. Daddy used to call him "little Bubba," and the name just stuck. From then on, everyone started calling him "Bubba."

I would recruit Bub to be my dancing partner. We would practice in our basement. I would swing him around and fling him in the air just as I had seen on the dance show on TV. He would oblige and follow my lead.

"No, you have to spin around first and then throw your arms high," I would tell him. "Ok, now look." I would demonstrate it again. "You got it?"

"Yea."

I'd promise to take him to the candy store if he learned my dance moves.

"You promise?"

"I said yeah, didn't I? Now stop complaining. Last time, and then we'll go. Just get it right, ok? Hit the music."

Bub put the needle on the record, and we performed in our imaginary talent show as the terrific two.

I called, "Darice, Darice come here! I want you to see something."

Running down the stairs, she said, "What?"

"Ok, you play the record and watch our routine."

"You called me for that?"

"We want you to see something."

She carefully placed the needle on the record and took a seat on our winding stairs. Bub did the spin just like I taught him. We grabbed hands and twirled. He slid through my legs with a leap off the floor. It was fantastic! What a dramatic ending! Out of breath, I quizzed Darice, "How was it?"

Unmoved, she looked at both of us and haughtily replied, "Stupid!" She turned and went back up the stairs.

I looked at Bub and said, "Forget her. She wouldn't recognize great talent if it knocked her in her head. Come on, let's go to the candy store."

Bub could care less about the dance. All he wanted to do was go to the store. He grabbed his loose change and stuffed it in his pockets. The store was right up the street, about two blocks away. It was already dark outside because of daylight saving time, so we knew we had to make it quick. So, Bub and I ran up the block to the store.

Upon entering the store, we were greeted at the door with a strong presence of incense and oils. The store always had a strange vibe to it—like it was left over from a 1970's time capsule. There were long beads that separated the front from the back of the store, and mirrors hung diagonally on every wall. A thick, red shaggy rug covered the floor and album covers decorated the corridor. A small corner of the store was devoted to selling chips and candy to the kids.

It was rumored they also sold grown-up things that most kids had no idea what they were. We would look at the oddly shaped apparatus behind the enclosed glass case and just stare inquisitively. We had no idea what the objects were used for. One of the owners always wore sunglasses even at night and spoke in long rhythmic melodic sentences. Yet, he was awfully kind to us indecisive kids who frequented his store. It was a peculiar place, as was the store's name. It was called Pleasure Unlimited. Now let that sink in for a moment. As kids, we thought it meant, unlimited candy and candy, unquestionably, brought us pleasure.

There were about five people inside. I got my Now & Laters, Nut Chews, and Blow Pops. Bub got his Snicker and his penny strawberry cookies.

As we were leaving, Bub said, "I wanna get something else."

"Hurry up," my look of agitation was now showing.

I repeated myself, "Hurry up." I shook my head in total frustration.

"Ok."

I glanced at the albums behind the glass case and then at the beads swinging from the doorway. Every time the door opened, the wind would cause a kaleidoscope of multi-hanging colors. I sensed an odd feeling, like something was out of place. There was an unusual connection to bad energy in the store. It swelled inside my belly, and I couldn't quite figure out what was happening. I anxiously knew it was best if we left the store immediately. I thought, "*It's time to go, now!*"

"Bub, let's go. Let's go, now!"

"Ok, I only want one more thing."

The bottom of my stomach continued to stir. I glanced at the owner, who had moved to the other side of the store near the vinyl records. He was servicing an adult customer. My eyes followed their transaction while darting back and forth to Bub, who was next in line to pay for his stuff. I sighed heavily because I could literally feel a weird energy consuming the entire place. It was clearly a premonition that something was about to happen. Electric waves had moved from my stomach up to my beating chest. Within seconds, "*Pop, Pop!*" There were two distinct sounds. Frightened, I reached and grabbed Bub. I pulled him to my chest, trying to block his view from what was happening. I knew it was a gunshot. I softly exhaled, "*I knew it.*"

"Nobody move!" the robber declared! The two gunshots caused the owner to fall backward behind the counter, hitting the floor. Bub tried to look up, and I held him firmly. I wanted to protect him by shielding his face from the commotion. I thought to myself, "*I knew we should have left.*" I could tell something was about to happen a split second before it did. It was in the air, and I don't know how, but I clearly sensed it. He pointed the gun at this tall boy who went to my school.

"You!"

The boy was scared. "Me?"

"You, open the register!"

The boy jumped over the counter and just started pushing buttons. He had no idea how to open it, so he continually pressed numbers until the drawer eventually opened. The rest of us in the store literally froze. I kept Bub close. We were in complete shock! The boy jumped out the way, and the robber grabbed the money and ran out of the store.

Thankfully, the robber didn't do anything to us, but as a kid, how do you process what just happened. It felt like thirty minutes had passed by, but the whole situation probably took only a few quick minutes. An older guy walked over and peered behind the counter and said, "Shit, he's good and dead." Bub couldn't breathe from me squeezing him tight. So, I finally loosened my grip to allow his oxygen to flow. The older guy took charge and said, "Wait, before anybody goes out. He might still be out there." We stayed inside for another seven minutes. Nobody uttered a word. We just waited. Then he tipped outside, looking both ways, up and down the street for any signs of the robber. He said, "I think it's ok for us to leave now." I grabbed Bub, and we ran top speed all the way home.

Growing up in the church, I recall how the pastor often spoke on the importance of honoring our ancestors and respecting the elders in the building. I loved how vividly he would explain that generationally, we are to pour into the younger generation to build them up. He would preach, "By doing so, you're paying homage to the many people who came before you. There's really no greater service than this. No one becomes whatever or whoever they're destined to become on their own. It's by design; we all have people in our lives who have helped us along the way."

This got me thinking about how my siblings, friends, and teachers all helped contribute to who I am today because of the major role they played in my life. Each one of them, in their very own selfless way, aided in my development. Accompanying me to dance class is just one example. Were they interested in dance? Nope, not hardly. But they would sit patiently and simply wait until I finished, never ever complaining. This self-sacrificing deed allowed me to safely travel to and fro doing something I love. I'm forever indebted to them.

Teresa is a cousin on my mother's paternal side. You wouldn't know that she's a year younger because she was indoctrinated by the streets. Explosive, brash, defiant, those are the qualities that embodied Teresa. Attitudinal with a short fuse, she could literally go from zero to one hundred in a nano of a second. She was everything I wasn't or could ever pretend to be. As a wise-cracking gentle giant, Teresa had very few home boundaries or so it seems. Polar opposites, no one believed we were related. Nonetheless, she adored her Kuykendal cousins, and we adored her. On some Saturday afternoons, Teresa would be gracious enough to travel with me to class. We would ride the bus together, and she would wait on the bench until I finished some three hours later. On our way home, we would almost always stop at the corner store for fries, candy, or both. The walk from Sammy Dyer to the L station was about six blocks. The store was somewhere in between.

I asked, "You know what you are getting?"

"Fries with sauce."

This week I decided on chips and a pop. There were two people in line as we waited for her order. It was a brisk sunny day even though old snow was still on the ground. The weather was finally breaking towards spring. I waited outside and looked at the massive apartment buildings up and down Cermak Avenue. Ma said they were called projects and people lived on top of each other in those buildings. The only time I heard the word "project" was on my favorite TV show, *Good Times*. They lived in the projects and always complained about their living conditions. I wondered if they complained all the time, too. It was how Ma said the word, *"projects,"* that indicated it was something less than desirable. She said I needed to be extra careful when passing by them. Safety was paramount. This is why someone always had to travel with me when I took the bus and the L. Honestly, I never felt anything when walking by the buildings. To me, they were tall, concrete, identical-looking buildings jammed next to each other.

Teresa finally emerged from the store clutching a grease-soaked paper bag. She murmured, "They're so slow."

"Yea, come on," I agreed. We crossed the street as we normally did, walking straight ahead to catch the L train. We stuffed greasy fries in our mouths, cracked jokes, and enjoyed our Saturday afternoon. A car pulled up and suddenly stopped right near us on the street. The driver rolled down the window.

"Where y'all going?"

It was if the world froze. We stopped in our tracks and didn't say a word at first. "Huh?" I said. The car would probably be described as a beater—an older-looking automobile.

The voice spoke again, but this time we were able to peek inside and see a female's face. She sounded anxious. "Where y'all going?" she asked again, this time sounding apprehensive. "Look, y'all don't know me, but I'm pretty sure those boys who were at the back of the store are coming for y'all. I overheard one of them say, "They were gonna catch yall."

What was this lady talking about? We turned around, and there were about four to five boys running in our direction. I still wasn't sure if they were chasing us or maybe running somewhere else. And if they were after us, then, why? Teresa didn't say a word. She followed my lead. I managed to say, "Up the street to the L."

"Hurry, get in. I'll drive y'all there. I don't know why but they definitely chasing you two. I heard them say it back at the store."

In a split second, a childhood image popped in my head, *"Do not talk to strangers. Do not talk to strangers!"* And now this stranger was telling us to get in her car? We looked again, and they were still running towards us. We jumped in the car, secretly praying that it was the right decision. Teresa got in the back, and I quickly got in the front. *"Dear Lord, please let this lady not be a serial killer on the hunt for two young girls, Amen."*

The lady sped off, driving us the remaining four blocks to the L. She pulled over, and we got out, repeatedly saying, "Thank you. Thank you!" while we were thinking, *"Thank you for not being a kidnapping ax murderer."*

"Please be careful," she said, and pulled off.

We ran as fast as we could up the fifty set of stairs to the L platform. Fortunately, we saw the lights of a train approaching. We kept looking back at the stairs, hoping they wouldn't make it to us before the train arrived. Finally, the train got to our stop, and the doors opened. We constantly looked at the top of the stairs in complete fear. We grabbed a seat. Within minutes, the doors closed, and we saw the group of boys hopping the turnstiles still running. Still trying to catch our breath, we were in disbelief of what just occurred. We rode in silence all the way home. This traumatic event left me with mixed feelings about whether I was going to return to Sammy Dyer the next dance season.

I thought about that lady a lot—the stranger who went out of her way to protect two little girls from harm.

She was an angel, sent from heaven to protect us on that fateful day. I told my sister what happened, but my cousin and I made a pact not to tell our parents because they would forever forbid us from traveling solo. That would have been the end of my newfound independence. I also kept my secret from them because I loved dance too much, and I knew they would have ended my dream of being a dancer. I held on to the promise of keeping our story hidden from the two people whose ultimate job was to keep me safe.

Truthfully, I never got over that Saturday afternoon. I used to appreciate the freedom of my self-governance, but everything changed after that. I now became anxious and uneasy during my travel. The paranoia became real. What if they're still looking for us? What would have happened if they had actually caught us? What if the lady hadn't been there? My mind was full of these preoccupied thoughts. I stopped being that free precocious child. And while I continued my training, I soon started researching new dancing schools. I lasted only a few more months at Sammy Dyer. It was definitely time for a change.

THE DIFFERENCE

Chapter VI – Adrienne

"**M**a, I think it's time for me to change dancing schools."

"Ok, now tell me why? I thought you really liked it there?"

"Well, I do. I mean, I did. It's kind of far, and now they want me in advance acrobats' class during the week. It's just a lot, plus it'll be getting dark early and trying to get there right after school, it'll be hard." It was all a lie.

"So, where are you gonna go?"

"I don't know yet. I'm still looking."

"Oh, ok." My parents were the complete anti-stage mom and dad. They pretty much let me soar and guided me when necessary. I never told them what happened. I wanted to move onward and as far away as possible. The world was a lot bigger and crueler than I imagined.

As usual, I took to the yellow pages and scouted the letter D for Dance. I searched through dance costumes, dance recitals, dance venues, dance lessons, dancing schools, and stopped at instruction—starting with the A's. I called about ten places asking, "What type of dance do you offer? I'm fifteen years old. Where are you located? How much is tuition? Do you have performing recitals?" I took careful notes because I was determined to find a new dance home that was closer and safer.

The high-pitched lady on the phone asked, "How old are you? Have you ever danced before?" There was a lot of noise in the background. "I can't hear you; can you please repeat that?" The lady sounded preoccupied. She said, "You can take a class for five dollars to see if you like it. We recommend ballet on Saturdays at 10:30 am." I was elated and wrote down the address. "Ma! Ma!" I called out. This dance school said I could take a class for five dollars to see if I like it. Is 7542 S. Cottage Grove far?"

I packed my dance bag with my ballet shoes but chose to wear my tights and

leotard under my jeans. I even threw my chiffon skirt in my bag for a little character.

"Ma, I only have to take one bus, right?" I took methodical notes. Ma looked at me with a quizzical expression that read, *"Who are you questioning?"*

"Yes!" She repeated the directions, "Take the 79th Street bus to Cottage Grove and walk three blocks north and look for the address."

"North? Is that to the right or left?"

"Left child!"

"Ok, I got it."

I was excited about this new energy I was feeling. The bus ride was easy, like a Sunday morning. I asked the bus driver, "Would you please call out Cottage Grove?" He smiled without saying a word, and I took a window seat.

In a loud, ostentatious voice, the bus driver called, "Next stop, Cottage Grove."

I walked to the front and politely said, "Thank you," and exited the bus. *"North, North? Ok, Ma said three blocks to the left, and I'll be heading north.* Public school had definitely failed me. I walked the block looking for 7542. I heard noise and music as I slowly pushed the front door open. The sounds grew louder, and a little girl practically knocked me over running out the door to an awaiting car. I entered and glanced at the pictures on the wall. Unlike Sammy Dyer, these were not famous celebrities of the past. Instead, they were of young girls and boys; I'm assuming students of the studio. The costumes clearly looked like an annual recital with uniformed shimmering metallic gold and sequin costumes. In one picture, the dancers were dressed as aliens. In another picture, the toddlers were in tutus. I always loved gazing at dance studio pictures because they contained the history and legacy of what came before. Oftentimes, they told a narration of the creative process.

"There's a girl out there," I heard a soft voice say.

"HELLO!!!" a coarse voice bellowed.

I was about to knock on the class door when I heard giggles.

"Turn the knob. Its open."

"Hi, I'm here for class. I called this week."

"Are you the one who went to Sammy Dyer?"

"Yes."

Children were everywhere. They were whizzing in and out of the studio. Some with juice pouches, others with greasy fries, chips, and candy. The only adult in the room was a tall, lanky lady who introduced herself as "Adrienne." She didn't seem to mind the commotion one bit. "You can put your things in the back room and change in the dressing room that also doubles as a bathroom." The girls laughed.

I could already tell Adrienne's personality was as tall as she was. She surely had to be at least six feet tall with a long-legged skinny body. She wore wide black spectacles, bright red lipstick, and an oversized sweatshirt that covered her leotard and tights. Her hair was unkempt, and she was loud, very loud. I soon discovered she was also very funny.

This space was instantly different from Sammy Dyer's. Aesthetically, it lacked the haughtiness, structure, and uniformity. You would have never been allowed to eat fries, let alone drink juice while walking across the studio floor. That was forbidden. Nor would dancers have the autonomy to speak so cavalier to the head Ballet Mistress. You couldn't even imagine taking a class in non-mono-chromatic leotard and tights in lieu of your personal style. It wasn't going to happen ever. However, this wasn't Kansas, and it surely wasn't Sammy Dyer.

I was now in Adrienne's universe, and my first impression was that everyone seemed familiar, like a family. Adrienne's smile was infectious and transmissible. The space was warm and caring. Her laugh was not only raucous; it was adorably genuine, all composed within a pure sweet spirit. I thought it odd that we didn't address her as Ms. Brazile or Ms. Adrienne, but far from being pretentious, she said, "Call me Adrienne." Her only requirements were hard work. With infectious energy and an eclectic personality, she was unlike any other human being I've ever met. Deciding to dance under her tutelage was one of the best decisions I've ever made.

I walked back through the door around 2:00 pm, a couple of hours later than my parents expected.

"Where have you been?" Ma inquired.

"I was still at dance. After ballet, Adrienne asked if I wanted to stay for the jazz class."

"Who's Adrienne?"

"She owns the studio, and she teaches all the classes. That's why I'm late. I actually took two classes but only had to pay for one class."

"Did you like it?"

"It's so different from Sammy Dyer. Adrienne is funny, not as strict and dry as Sammy Dyer. I mean, we're learning technique and stuff, but it's way more fun."

How much is tuition?" These were the important questions Ma needed to know.

"Thirty-five dollars per month with unlimited classes. Not bad, right?"

"I think we can swing that."

"Adrienne said I can bring the first thirty-five dollars next Saturday if I start."

"Ok, I'll talk to your dad, and see what he says. Hey?" I turned around. "I can't wait until you start making all this money to pay us back."

"Oh, Ma, now you know I got y'all! Imma be rich!" Ma's smile was worth a thousand words. She was my biggest cheerleader.

It was a one-stop-shop. I caught a single twenty-minute bus ride to my new dancing school, and besides, I felt safe. I was quickly getting comfortable at the studio and was adjusting to my new teacher's style of discipline, or lack thereof. It was beginning to feel like home. Though I have to admit this was not the class structure I was accustomed, so it took some time for me to get used to it. As a matter of fact, I loathed disorganization. I soon realized and appreciated how serious I took my study. Don't get me wrong, as a fifteen-year-old, I'd enjoyed acting silly and having just as much fun as the next teenager who was on the cusp of puberty. However, when it came time to focus and concentrate on things that were important to me, I was all business. I never truly adapted to the loose environment very well. I think this skill was innate, just who I am as a person.

While other dancers would rush across the street for the greasy bag of fries during break time, I'd stay contently at the barre, stretching my arabesque or practicing choreography. I remained quiet and zealous about my art, and my technique improved. I didn't go out my way to become besties with the other dancers, but I was congenial. I didn't go to make friends; I went to study dance. I was perfectly fine being labeled an outsider. Most of the girls had been dancing together for at least five years, and as the new kid on the block, I wasn't the slightest interested in cliques. Besides, I found it strange that each girl would constantly remind you of how many years they've been studying dance. My brief three years of instruction paled in comparison, which made me question their under-developed technique. The point of studying anything is to get better at it, right? This was my sole goal—to grow and improve in ballet and to one day transition to en pointe class.

Kim was the studio diva. She was beautiful, and her eyes matched the sandy color of her hair. I labeled her diva not because she possessed a dramatic, selfish temperament, but because everyone thought she was the best dancer at the studio. It was in no way reflective of her personality. She was nice and friendly, and she was a good dancer.

My mindset wanted more, demanded more, and as a result, I gave more of myself in my training. I didn't strive to be better than anyone at Adrienne's. This internal competition pushed me to take my skill to the next level. I noticed, at times, my reserved personality made others uncomfortable. In class, the girls would often giggle and keke at private jokes. I took no offense and remained engrossed in deep concentration. My memory was sharp as I could catch choreography on the first and second try of it being taught. And during rehearsals, when we were allowed to "walk-through" the choreography to preserve our energy, it was mostly a full-out performance from me. I was very hard on myself if my double or triple pirouette failed. I'd keep trying and trying until I would finally get it.

"Patrice, fall forward when you spin; you're falling backward. The weight should always be on the balls of your foot," Adrienne would tell me. She was a good teacher. Very patient and hilarious. She kept us bowled over in laughter, even when providing constructive criticism. It was hard to take her seriously.

"Ughhh, ok, let me try again." I would work on every corrective note Adrienne gave me. Her aura made her very approachable, and I'd ask reflective questions at the end of class. "When do you think I'll be able to go on pointe?" I asked her.

"Well, let's keep up with the ballet lessons, because I want to make sure your ankles are strong enough," Adrienne would say over and over. This went on for about five months. It made me more determined to master the beauty and pain of having strong ankles. It has always been my dream to one day dance in satin pink-covered toe shoes.

The summer months were the off-season. However, there was no off-season for me. I practiced everywhere, in the living room, even in the aisles of the grocery stores. I was forever pliéing, reléveing, and sus-sousing all day long. I continued my practice.

I returned to Adrienne in the fall when the new school year began. I was happy to be back and eager to learn more. The strength of my calf muscles began to bulge through my tights as I warmed up my body. I looked around and noticed class had grown. There were more contemporary dancers sprinkled among the veterans. I was anxious to start, so I concentrated on aligning my spine and correcting my posterior while Adrienne recited her welcome back greeting. My limbs were now loose and nimble. "Would she stop talking already?" I thought silently. "We're wasting valuable dance time." My eyes scan the room to see if anyone else is annoyed.

"I want to welcome my new dancers as well as the familiar faces to the start of a new dance season," Adrienne began. "I want us to go to competitions this year and bring home some first-place trophies. We have two new students, Jane and Yolanda. They are sisters."

Jane was the better dancer of the two, but neither girl stuck around very long after the initial introduction.

Adrienne continued, "Since this is a new season, we're going to have some rules." All eyes darted about, fixated on what she was about to say.

Kimberly W. blurted, "What?"

While another dancer rolled her eyes and sucked her teeth. I would have never expressed my disdain aloud. I was not that bold or vocal.

Adrienne did not address the disrespect. "Yes, dearie. Rules. No eating in the studio, and do not walk across the floor in your little, ugly street shoes."

One girl jokingly interrupted, "My shoes not ugly. They cost almost a hunnid dollaz."

"May I finish?" Adrienne's sarcasm was on full display. The girl rolled her eyes. "Take them off at the door. If you wanna get any food, you'll have to wait until class is completely over, and then go across the street to get y'all fries and whatnot. I am serious this time."

The fact that she had to say she was serious, only meant, that she really wasn't.

"We need to start treating this space like a respectful studio." There were a few more hisses and yawns, but everyone knew she was just too nice to be an enforcer of rules and order. "Any questions?" No one said a word. "Ok, then everyone at the barre." The girls all moved as if they were just issued a death sentence. By the end of class, Adrienne motioned for my attention. I packed up and walked over.

"Yes, Adrienne."

"Ok, Missy, your ankles and legs are looking strong. I think it is time for you to take ballet on pointe."

I let the words sink in. *"Did she just say I'm ready for my first pair of toe shoes?"*

"I want you to get fitted for Bloch toe shoes." My hard work was paying off. She scribbled the name of a company that specializes in dance shoes and handed the paper to me.

"Try to have them for class next week."

"Oh, I'll have them for sure!"

I rushed home after class to share this whirlwind of a proclamation. "Daddy, I gotta get dancing shoes for ballet class. Adrienne said my ankles and legs are finally ready for toe shoes." My father just looked at me, not knowing what I was talking about.

He simply said, "When do you need them?"

"For class next Saturday."

"Ok, we'll get them one day after school." I trusted his every word.

A few days later, Daddy and I made the trek downtown to the Wabash Dance Company. Daddy hated driving downtown because he said there was never affordable parking.

The man inside the store was an older gentleman. He knelt beside the chair and measured my foot. He asked, "First pair?"

"Yes. I was told to get Bloch. Do you have them?"

"We sure do," he exclaimed! He finished measuring both feet. "I'll be right back."

My father was a man of few words with a domineering presence. We waited for the salesman to return.

"I think these will do." He picked up a foamy pad and loose material of some sort.

"What's that?"

"Oh, this? This right here is lamb's wool, and these things are called toe pads. First, you lightly wrap the lamb's wool around the toes, then cover them with a toe pad. It cups the ball of your toes like a hat."

"What does it do?"

"The wool and pad are an extra cushion of protection. Feel this." He handed me one of the shoes.

"Wow! This is really hard."

The salesman took the shoe and used it to bang on the floor, making a loud thumping sound.

This did not at all appear to be the same shoes I've studied so many times in books or seen on television—the soft, grace-swan-like-slipper. The loud noise even broke Dad's silence.

"That thing sure is hard. You sure you're getting the right shoes?" dad asked.

"Yes, it's her first pair, and they're all like this. She will learn how to break them in, so they will conform to her feet. The material and wood underneath will provide a new dancer with the support without breaking her ankles or crushing her toes as she slips, spins, slides, and even falls within the graceful world of ballet."

We continued with my fitting. There was so much to learn and discover. After wrapping the ribbon around my ankle, the salesman tied the ends into little knots and stuffed the excess ribbon into the sides of the shoes. Sarcastically he said, "Wouldn't want you to trip and fall over this pretty pink ribbon, would we?" He finally directed me to stand. He looked at my dad, "Don't worry! They're not supposed to feel like walking shoes. How are your toes, dear? Is it too much wool inside?"

I honestly didn't know how to answer. "Uh, ok, I guess."

"Well, you can always remove some of the lamb's wool if you like. That's your call. You can use as much or less as you want until you become more comfortable in them."

I smiled at my dad. He looked at the salesman, "Will she need anything else?"

"Nope, that's it."

Dad paid for the shoes and we headed back to the confines of the southside.

THE DIFFERENCE

Chapter VII – Shenanigans

In class, Adrienne taught me how to break in my shoes, literally. She banged them against the wall and the floor to make them more flexible, bending them forward and backward several times over. Monday night was now added to my dance schedule. This night was dedicated strictly to pointe class. Ballet was still taught on Saturdays, but pointe was for the more advanced dancers. Since Darice had started driving, Ma would let her drive me to my pointe class.

In the winter season, it began to get dark around 4:00 pm, and Ma and Daddy didn't want me on the bus at night. Darice and her partner in crime, Gwen, would drive me to dance. Even though Gwen's Mom was more strict than our Mom, she would allow Gwen to ride with us. People said

Gwen looked like us and could have easily been another sister. She and Darice had been friends since middle school. Gwen was, without a doubt, boy crazy, which is probably why her parents didn't allow her to venture too far away, or maybe it had something to do with the fact that they were devout Jehovah's Witnesses. Which kind of explains why Gwen adored spending so much time at our house. Our parents were never suffocating and allowed us to grow independently.

Imagine three carefree teenagers driving, hanging out, flirting with boys, having innocent and sometimes not so innocent fun. I admit, I was the least boy crazed of them all. Don't get me wrong, I thought they were super cute, but it didn't go too far beyond that. On the days we were allowed to drive, Darice and Gwen would wait for me, parked in front of the studio, listening to music, cracking jokes, basically doing anything to pass the time. However, on some days after I entered the studio, Lord only knows where they went. I could probably guess; they were somewhere visiting boys. As long as they were back by the time I finished class, it was cool. They were fast hormonal teenage girls who liked boys, and by that, I mean a lot!

During one of their hot girl adventures, they dropped me off for my pointe class. When I finished class at 7:15 pm, they were not outside. The longer I waited, the more agitated I became. I looked at my watch; it was 7:25 pm. *"Where are they?"* I thought. Ten more minutes passed as I looked up and down the street for Ma's white Ford Escort to be turning the corner on two wheels. Five more minutes elapsed. I checked the time again, 7:30 pm. It was officially on, and I schemed of a way to pay them back for making me wait. I decided to walk to the bus stop and catch the bus home. They will have to face the music when I walk in the house alone, prepared to snitch. I was heated and prepared to tell it all. Whatever trouble they endure will be worth it. *"How dare they leave me stranded?"* And as a result, I wanted them to sustain the wrath of Mary and James Kuykendal.

I hopped off the bus around 8:00 pm and orchestrated my plan. I finally made it home about ten minutes later. "Ma, Darice here?" Hence, I knew she wasn't, and she probably was going crazy looking for me.

"What you mean? Isn't y'all together?"

"No. They didn't pick me up. I ended up catching the bus home."

"WHAT! Where are they?"

"Ma, I don't know. They dropped me off and left." My plan was working.

"Left? What do you mean they left?"

Less than ten minutes later, Darice and Gwen tried to sneak through the front door. I was sitting at the table, pretending to still be in a funk. Ma went in. "Where were you two?"

Darice started with a lie but couldn't finish it. I sat there gloating on the inside while pretending to appear pathetic on the outside.

Ma repeated herself, "Where were you two?"

I tried to explain dolefully, "Ma, I waited for like thirty minutes." (*I lied. It was more like fifteen minutes*). "Adrienne had to lock up." (*She didn't, I lied again*). "That's why I had to catch the bus because she had somewhere to go."

Gwen coyly interjected, "Ms. Kuykendal, I have to get home."

Ma interrupted, "What you have to do is sit your little fast ass right there and tell me what happened, or do I have to call your dad, Mr. Matthews?"

Gwen's effort in trying to sly her way out the door failed miserably. Besides, Mary Kuykendal wasn't having it. Gwen slinked down and took a seat at the table next to Darice.

Ma continued. "You two are the older ones. Do you know how dangerous that little stunt was? I mean for Christ Sakes!" It was eerily quiet. Ma was clearly worried, and here I was, just being ornery. Exasperated, Ma walked out of the room.

Gwen lived three blocks away. She slowly got up, not sure if the disciplining was over. "Good night, Ms. Kuykendal." She walked home praying Ma did not call her dad to tell him about tonight's fiasco.

Darice didn't speak to me for two days, which felt like a lifetime when you share a bedroom together. It was a pain, but I took the bus to dance the following week. Darice finally slowly started speaking to me again, and all was forgiven with the Kuykendal siblings. Believe it or not, Ma even allowed Darice to start driving me again on Monday nights.

I don't think Ma ever told Daddy about that night. Sometimes, I sit back and reflect on parenting. No matter how many times a child disappoints their parents, they're always forgiven, and they are there for them until the end. We were lucky to have those types of parents because we were right back to our daily shenanigans. As you will see, we hadn't learned a thing from that night. Remember, I mentioned how boy crazy frick and frack were, right? You're not going to believe what they did next. Let me further expound.

"Ma, we leaving," I yelled. Gwen was already outside, waiting for us. I hopped in the backseat. Gwen took the front so the two of them could finish their daily high school gossip.

Darice turned to me, "We're not going to dance today."

"Like she's ever been in a dance class," I thought. "Huh?" I questioned.

"We're going to Pill Hill," Darice said, locking eyes with mine in the rear-view mirror. Pill Hill was an area on the southeast side surrounded by huge elaborate houses with parochial–schooled boys. I knew something was up because Gwen instantly started laughing uncontrollably.

"Nah, I have to go, sister sledge." I tried to reason with the hooligans.

Darice said, "We're early. We will go just for a minute, and then we'll leave."

Shaking my head, I slapped my forehead with my palm and sank in the backseat. I have to admit, hanging with Thelma and Louise was more spontaneous and fun. Truth be told, my hormones were raging, which made me want to hang out a little too. Being careful not to implicate herself too deeply, Gwen just innocently smiled and laughed as if this wasn't her idea. We drove right past our regular right turn to my dancing school. I blurted, "If we get caught..."

Darice fired back, "Shut up! We not gonna get caught unless you..." Her voice trailed off. They snarked a mean glare and growl in my direction. Darice said, "Matter of fact, we're taking you over Skip's house."

"Skip! No!" Skip was the quintessential spoiled Mama's boy, who at age fifteen, wore everything Gucci to school. He liked me and was really cute. His dog was even named Gucci. I mean, he could really dress, and yes, just like so many other "Pill-Hill" boys, he went to an all-boys catholic school. The only difference was that these boys took communion at school in the presence of priests and nuns. *"NO! DO.NOT.GO. TO.HIS.HOUSE"* My heart was beating. I pleaded, "Do NOT go to his house!!!" I demanded. I was adamant.

They thought this was a hilarious idea. Gwen could no longer contain herself. She laughed so hard; she spit out her pop.

"I'm not playing. Don't go over to his house."

Darice turned down his block. Skip was standing outside. I'm thinking, *"I am going to die, literally, F**ing Die right here, right now."* She slowed the car and rolled down her window, "Hey Skip." I'd never understood how they were so comfortable around boys, especially cute ones. He peered and walked to the car.

"There's Patrice," Gwen motioned to the back seat.

"I'm dying; please save me, Lord."

"Hey, Patrice! Get out the car."

"I'm dead. Why me, Lord? Why me?" I knew this was a bad idea. A horrible idea. Laughing, they both looked at me. I murmured, "Don't leave." I mustered the courage to get out of the car.

As soon as the door closed, the tires screeched, burning rubber, emitting a light smoke. They peeled down the block leaving us standing in the middle of the street. I re-peated to myself, *"Please save me, God! Save me, God. Save me, God. Save me, God."* We sat on his porch, thinking they would be right back. You know, scare me a little and then quickly come back around to take me to class. Ten minutes passed, and he invited me inside. I felt safe when he introduced me to his mother. *Good, his mom is home.* We went to his room, and he closed the door. Instantly, he tried to kiss me. I ducked and dodged, reminding him, "Your mom is in the next room."

"She knows we're in here," Skip said.

"Please save me, God! Save me, God. Save me, God. Save me, God." He turned into an octopus—reaching, grabbing, feeling, and touching. Every time I slapped one hand away, here comes another one. "I need to go. They're probably back outside." Embarrassed as we passed his mother, I managed an awkward politeness, "Nice meeting you, Ma'am." He grabbed my hand, and we went back out-side.

It felt like an hour had passed, but I knew it had only been only maybe twenty minutes. It was too late to go to dance class now. We made forcible small talk waiting for the dynamic duo to return. Finally, I saw the Escort pull into the driveway. I got in the car incensed.

Darice yelled, "See ya', Skip," and screeched down the block.

Infuriated, "It's too late for me to go now. What took y'all so long? Do y'all know his mom was in the next room, and he still tried to kiss and feel me up? Ughh! I can't believe it. Adrienne's going to kill me! Now I'm behind and have to learn whatever she taught today." I grabbed my face with both hands and let out a sigh of doom, collapsing on the backseat.

While it was indeed an adventure, I felt horrible at the same time. I sacrificed something I loved, and for what? Absolutely nothing. I thought about the choreography I missed and how I'd have to play catch up next week. I always took my study seriously, and here I just blew it off like no big deal. This was a hard lesson. One that I didn't want to participate in again. I let myself down. It was at this moment that I realized the significant role dance played in my world.

I enjoyed learning under Adrienne. This year's recital was comprised of an ode to Cinderella. I was sure Kim would have been given the coveted role to play Cinderella. However, Adrienne announced, "Anyone interested in playing Cinderella must audition. You must dance on pointe, and the audition will take place in two weeks."

This news thrilled me! I loved the challenge, and pointe was by far no easy feat. I wanted my audition to stand out, so I stepped up my training by experimenting with new ballet combinations merging dance genres. I loved the soulful association performed by Alvin Ailey. I started to emulate how they would use a range of emotions to blend with their movement. You could almost *feel* the heartbeat of their choreography. It was refreshing! Ballet was more subdued, and modern dancing was an art connected to storytelling. I was determined to win the role of Cinderella.

My commitment stretched to learning about the myriad styles of performances, dance companies, and dancers who paved the way. In my research, I stumbled upon beautiful faces that resembled mine. What a phenomenal discovery of cultural impressions of Josephine Baker and Katherine Dunham. I learned how they traveled the world both domestically and internationally, weaving their artistic stories. Then there was Arthur Mitchell, who was a visionary, and how he showed the world that black is not only beautiful but that our talent is undeniable. Mr. Mitchell became the first black male dancer to perform with the New York City Ballet. All this knowledge was inspiring. He dispelled the myth that black bodies were not biologically apt to become ballerinas.

Mr. Mitchell wanted to make an impact in American ballet by establishing the Dance Theatre of Harlem in 1969—a genre that often ignored and excluded African American talent from being showcased. I read every piece of literature I could find on Mr. Mitchell. I studied the photographs, the faces, and the lines of their beautiful bodies. This placed me on a quest to discover more. As a result, I was soon led to Alvin Ailey and the majestic royalty of Judith Jamison. Ailey's style was deeply embedded within the narrative of the black soul and the black church. I got chills looking at the lines of Ms. Jamison and the stories her dance told without using a single word.

Rooted in the black experience, these pieces were created by us, for us, and then for the entire world to enjoy and appreciate. The more I uncovered faces that emulated mine, the easier it was for me to conceptualize myself in those spaces. From there, a moxie of a performer named Debbie Allen was busy studying in the halls of Howard University, a historically black college. She was prepping for her Broadway performance of Sweet Charity. Ms. Allen commanded attention when she entered a room. On a television show, she captured my attention when she recited the infamous lines, "You want Fame? Well, Fame cost. And right here is where you start paying in sweat." Those words forever stuck with me, and I never forgot them.

There were three of us who auditioned, and by the looks of it, only one who took it seriously. I was deliberate and intentional. I studied constantly and intensely. I was methodical in rehearsals, scrutinizing every rond de jambe and grand battement I performed. I didn't need a french-fry break. I didn't require a slushy moment. It was unprofessional and unnecessary. I wasn't the typical teenager. This was more than a fleeting hobby. I wanted to earn the coveted role with my technique and execution. I had goals. And *I* knew I was born to play this part. When my name was called and I was chosen for the part of Cinderella, tears filled the crevices of my eyes. *"This must be what joy feels like."* This was a big deal in my world.

Four years passed since I began studying with Adrienne. I watched girls leave, come back, have children, or just abandon dance altogether. I loved her deeply but decided it was time to leave her studio. Adrienne was a great teacher, but she had taught me all she knew, and for that, I was beyond grateful. And once again, it was time to expand my study. I needed to elevate my training.

I left the comfort of the southside to pursue my goals. I wanted to heighten my skills. Instead of doing a double pirouette, I longed for a triple, a quadruple. My leg extensions were now extending to 6:00, and still, I wasn't satisfied. I wanted to become a better dancer. I began to travel north to Evanston by train to take classes at Gus Giordano. The south/northbound Halsted bus took me to the Joseph Holmes Studio, where I trained as a summer apprentice. Later, in the Andersonville neighborhood, I discovered Joel Hall along with one of the hottest dancers in Chicago named Elaine, or E for short. She was from the westside and was both stunning on the inside and outside. Without hesitancy, she was by far the fiercest dancer I came to know. She taught dance in the park district and was affectionately known as Ms. Elaine by her students. Her park was within proximity to the Dome where Bob Richardson, a former Ailey protegee, was busily choreographing stunning pieces to the likes of Roberta Flack. I studied and learned from everyone. It didn't matter if it was on the north, south, or west side, downtown or uptown; I took classes everywhere.

THE DECISION

Chapter VIII – Keleila

After high school graduation, I decided to attend Western Illinois University because my counselor did a piss-poor job in securing post-secondary options. I had to go somewhere because not going was not an option. They accepted me, and all my friends were going there. I figured what did I have to lose?

Fall rolled around, and Daddy and I arrived on campus ready to unload my stuff into my dormitory. I was rooming with my best friend, Keleila. Everyone said it was the worse decision friends could make because it was doomed to fail, and we were guaranteed to fall apart. We disagreed and ignored the naysayers. We settled in quickly and nicely.

Keleila and I met junior year in high school. I became friends with her sister, Latrice, first in Spanish class. She later introduced me to Keleila. After meeting them, I said, "Wait, you're both in the same grade? You twins?"

They laughed. "No, we're not twins." Keleila said, "We're ten months apart."

I didn't know that was possible, but ok. "You've been in the same grade together forever?"

"Uh-huh, I have the late birthday," Latrice answered. Latrice was the more reserved one, while Keleila was the firecracker—who looked like Vanessa Williams, the first Black Miss America. She was boisterous, bold, and beautiful. They both were respectful and sweet, but Keleila was more opinionated and didn't have a problem speaking her mind and checking people when they needed to be checked. I admired that about her. On many occasions, her brassiness got us in a whole lot of trouble, especially in a hick town like Macomb, but I loved that about her.

I took a dance class on campus to keep me sane on an otherwise very boring, uneventful campus. One day walking through the school union, I saw a post looking for dancers to audition for the Gwendolyn Brooks Dance Troupe. Keleila decided to try out, too, even though she wasn't a trained dancer. I figured with very little social life happening within the cornfields of Interstate 55, this may be worth our interest.

Western was such a dry cornfield county. With only a handful of black folks, it was a predominately white college town. The dance troupe was housed in the art center in the Black Student Union. It was named after the first Black Poet Laureate of Illinois, Ms. Gwendolyn Brooks. The troupe consisted mainly of sorority girls and a few guys whose sole purpose was to legally rub up on girls for the sake of art. The females were either in their junior or senior year, and we were the doe-eyed freshmen.

A girl named Lisa was the captain. She was pompous and pretentious. She and her cronies would intimidate the new recruits, which was strange because we just wanted to dance. At the audition, Lisa made sure everyone knew she was in charge. She called for our attention. "We're going to teach you a combination and then break into groups. You'll have an opportunity to perform twice. The first will be the choreographed routine, and the second will consist of a personal dance of your own. Any questions?" Everyone was quiet. "Great!"

Keleila and I looked at each other and instantly knew what the other was thinking. Our eyes said it all, *"This Bitch."*

Lisa finished, "Everybody up. This will be the front." She faced and pointed to the mirrors.

A frail, thin white boy came and stood next to me. "What's your name?" he asked.

"Patrice."

"You learn really fast."

"Thanks, I used to dance back home."

"I'm Teddy." Teddy's personality was colorful. He was an interesting character. He was the only white guy auditioning to be on a historically black dance troupe. He earned respect based on merit alone.

"Teddy, you're next," said Lisa.

Keleila whispered, "What's this white boy doing here?"

I shushed her, "His name is Teddy. Let's see what he can do." Ten seconds into the music, I could feel the burning sensation of Keleila's eyes piercing into my soul, trying to make eye contact with me. I refused to look at her. Simply refused. Wouldn't do it. Couldn't do it. I knew the outcome. It wouldn't be pretty. It wouldn't be nice. We would both be on the floor hollering from laughter.

Teddy was HORRIBLE! He jerked and flailed his body like a floundering fish. He ended his routine with an imaginary whip of hair and sashayed off the floor. I watched, thinking, *"You got to be kidding?"*

Lisa took center floor. "Thank you for auditioning. Check in the union tomorrow around noon. If you make the team, your name will be posted on the student board." We gathered our things and headed out the door.

"Hey, wait up."

We turned around to find Teddy calling for us. Keleila said, "Oh my God, Patrice."

I whispered, "Be nice."

96

Teddy caught up with us. "I'm walking this way too. Mind if I join? Where y'all stay?"

"Washington."

"Oh cool, I'm at Lincoln." I introduced Keleila. "Teddy, this is Keleila."

"Hey Keleila, your eyes are so pretty. Are they green?"

"Yea, green in the summer and gray in the winter, thanks."

Teddy couldn't wait to talk about the auditions. He was definitely a talker. His flamboyant demeanor was, at times, over-the-top. However, you couldn't deny his genuine friendliness. The three of us walked back to the dorms laughing and chatting.

Teddy said, "You guys are so nice. I hope all three of us make the team. I mean, you both were really good. How do you think I did?"

We stopped dead in our tracks.

Teddy said, "What?"

Keleila blurted, "I'm sorry, Teddy, I have to be honest with you. You were completely horrible!" My eyes shifted to Teddy and after a second of silence, we busted out laughing.

"I know I'm not that good of a dancer, but I still want to dance. I love to dance!"

"Well, as long as you know."

"If I make it, hopefully, I'll get better." He sounded sincere as if his statement rebounded from a place of hurt.

I can only imagine some of the mean and hurtful comments that have been thrown his way. He was ultra-feminine with an innocent spirit. We crossed the yard leading us to our respective dorm entry.

"See you soon, hopefully at dance practice," Teddy yelled.

Keleila looked at me shaking her head. "You know there's no help for him. He was beyond awful. He's funny, he's nice, but he was the absolute worse! Patrice, now you KNOW he can't dance."

"Yes, but that's not our problem. Besides, the way those girls treated everyone, he's definitely not going to make the team." To be honest, I wasn't so sure if we were going to make it either. The dance was pretty easy, but those girls were vicious.

Keleila and I agreed to meet for lunch so we could look at the list together. I wasn't nervous. Not because I thought I was a shoo-in, but merely because I had been down this road before, and as they say, it wasn't my first rodeo. Keleila, on the other hand, was petrified. She ran up to me at the union. "You ready?" she asked.

"Yea."

She grabbed my arm, "Wait."

"Wait for what? I thought you were ready to look."

"I was, I mean, I am. Let's walk slow."

Oh, the dramatics, "Let's go." I pulled her by the arm as we headed down the corridor. A small group had formed as everyone looked for their name. The first person we noticed was Teddy. The only skinny blonde kid in the group.

"I made it! I made it!" Teddy squealed.

In pure disbelief, our mouths dropped open, and we darted to the board. Keleila and I had made the team too. As a matter of fact, everyone who tried out was chosen. We didn't know what to expect, but we figured it'd be fun and gives us something to do.

The team is comprised of fifteen members. There were ten girls, four guys, and Teddy. Our first practice was fun. Right away, we started bonding and learning choreography. We would eventually perform for the student body during homecoming and spirit week. This was exciting.

I was undecided on a career and hadn't yet declared an academic major. I was taking general humanity classes for the first year. The fraternity and sorority life were intriguing. I mean, I never saw myself as a sorority girl, but a particular group piqued my interest. Word on the yard was that the chapter got in trouble and was suspended from campus. My roommate and I often imitated the fraternities in our dorm room. We were hilarious.

College life consisted of parties, dancing, eating with a little studying. The freshmen gain of fifteen pounds quietly morphed into my physique. Standing at five feet ten, my figure went from slim to slim-thick. Ok, maybe not thick-thick, but you get the point.

During a visit from my sister and her boyfriend, a top-notch basketball recruit at Ohio State, both noticed the weight gain. He said, "Patrice, you've gained weight!"

Just as surprised as they were, I barely noticed the fifteen pounds. Extra weight is easy to camouflage in over-sized sweats. I responded, "I did?" Looking down at my body, I wasn't the least bit offended. He was just like a brother and had been in the family for a while. Thank God I didn't have body issues, so I just shrugged the whole revelation off. It was no big deal. What else are you supposed to do at 10:00 pm besides eat nachos and fries? Back home, my dance class would have been adequate exercise, but my new routine wasn't nearly enough. I decided to hit the gym to combat the freshmen fifteen.

I decided to take an economic class to try and find my life's purpose. I thought about investment banking. It didn't go well. I dropped the class. I thought, Maybe I could work in radio broadcasting. Working at a radio station sounded like fun. I took a broadcasting course. Yeah, Nah. I quickly lost interest.

Ironically, the one thing I thoroughly enjoyed never entered my conscience as a career. I was really good at dancing. Yet, I never thought of saying it aloud, *"I'll become a professional dancer."* I reminisced about the beautiful images of Ms. Allen, Ms. Jamison, Mr. Mitchell, and Alvin Ailey and thought of their lasting legacies. Subconsciously, maybe I didn't think I was good enough or that this could actually happen in real life for me. How does one even become a professional dancer? I didn't personally know anyone who actually made a living simply dancing. I watched my parents work. They provided. It's what you do. You get up every day and go to work. Dance wasn't work. It was an escape to have fun and do something you love, which is probably why I struggled to declare a major in college. I was utterly clueless.

Our rehearsals dramatically increased. The captain explained that every year during Black history month, the dance troupe would perform at a correctional facility sixty miles away in East Moline, Illinois. "Don't worry. It's a medium-security prison." She explained. Keleila raised her hand. "Yes, Keleila."

"So, will the inmates be behind bars when we dance?"

The veteran members chuckled in laughter. "No, they won't. There won't be any murderers or rapists or anyone like that. It's a low to medium-security detention facility, and believe it or not, it's a lot of fun."

I sighed, "Not."

All the new members sat there stunned in disbelief. A prison? We're dancing at a prison. Keleila whispered, "Dr. King would not approve of such debauchery."

I asked, "Do we know which routine we will perform?"

"Definitely, *'Push It'* by Salt n' Pepa will be one of them."

Teddy glanced over at me with his blue eyes bulging out of his eye socket. I leaned over and whispered, "Please tell me she did not just say we are performing *'Push It'* at a prison? Inmates who have been locked up for Lord knows how long. Please tell me that didn't just happen. How about a liturgical piece? To get them closer to the good word?"

Keleila laughed, "Yea, that's pretty much what she said."

I was trying to respect the old heads, but to prove my point, Keleila jumped up and did an over-the-top exaggerated pelvic thrust, mouthing the words, "Ahh, push it, push it *real* good." We cracked up.

"There will be nothing to worry about. We will be fine. Trust me. Now let's finish learning the rest of this choreography" said Lisa, We stood up.

I thought to myself, *"I sure hope she's right."*

The sponsor of the dance troupe was Ms. Williams, a faculty member of the university. She was an alumnus originally from Rockford, Illinois. As the team sponsor, she was required to travel with us on extended outings and activities. She referred to the prison outreach as ministering. I beg to differ.

On the day of our trip, we arrived at The Gwendolyn Brooks House very early. Our call time was 5:00 am. Felecia, a veteran dancer, was late and missed the trip altogether. She was on the program to perform a solo. Still trying to get the sleep out of our eyes, we quietly boarded a coach bus and took our seats.

"How are you girls feeling?" Lisa asked, sitting directly across from us. "This is your first road trip with the team."

I couldn't hide my trepidation and asked straight out. "You're sure there will be security?"

In her smug type of way, again, Lisa guaranteed there was nothing to worry about.

Keleila asked, "What about Felecia's part?"

"Actually, I was just about to ask Patrice if she would feel comfortable taking Felecia's solo?" By now everyone knew of my dance background, and I could improvise to any song.

"You want me to do Felecia's solo?" This was shocking news!

"No, I want you to perform your own piece."

Keleila whispered, "Oh P, you have to do it. You can dance circles around these Bitches, and by far, you're the best dancer on the team anyway."

I was never one to back away from a challenge. "Ok, I'll do it."

Lisa stood up and announced, "Excuse me everyone, since Felecia isn't here, Patrice has graciously decided to perform a solo in today's show." Everyone erupted with applause, and of course, the loudest applause came from my best friend, Keleila.

"What song are you using?" Keleila asked.

"I have the begging song on tape and was thinking about using that. What do you think?"

"By Lenny Williams?" Keleila broke out in her rendition, "Oh, Oh, Oh, Oh, Oh, Oh, Oh, Oh...Yea, that's a good one."

We finally arrived in East Moline at the medium-security prison. We passed through barb-wired gates. It became eerily quiet the closer we got to the building that housed the prisoners. Shit got real, really quick. We exited the bus and stayed close together. We were checked for contraband in the security line and handed a locker for our personal belongings. Two gentlemen were personally assigned to security detail and took us to the holding area for the performance. I handed Lisa a tape. "Here's my music. I'm doing the begging song by Lenny Williams, but I need to cue it."

"Dancers, make sure you stretch and warm up," Lisa instructed. "In about ten minutes, we're starting."

We entered the gymnasium. The inmates were already seated on bleachers. Lisa pointed, "This will be our front." She quickly ran through blocking without us having to take the floor. "We will face those rows, and unfortunately, anyone sitting on the side will get a peripheral view. It's the best we can do."

There had to be at least 300 people in attendance. You could feel their energy. They were definitely thrilled we were there! The uniformed crowd looked like a sea of blue and white in the stands. There were no gates, bars, ropes, or fences. Only two guards that were posted on opposing ends of the hall.

Keleila caught me staring at the audience. "Are you ok?"

I jerked my attention away from the crowd, alarmed. "Huh?" I paused and looked at my friend. She knew something was *really* bothering me.

"What?"

"Keleila?" I was becoming light-headed. "There's a guy out there that looks exactly like my uncle." I was having palpitations as my heart began to race. I hadn't seen my uncle in probably twenty years. Wasn't even sure what he looked like. Growing up, I remember ear-hustling and hearing the adults talk about him being in and out of jail, but as kids, you dared not inquire about grown folks' business. I shot a brief glance back at the crowd, and my eyes instantly locked with this man sitting on the end row.

"Where? Which one?"

For some weird reason, I didn't want to look again. I felt exposed as he was staring directly at me. If it was him, maybe he was thinking the same thing. I took another gander, and this time, the gentleman winked at me.

"He just winked, Keleila. That must be him, sitting on the end, all the way on the left, about the third row."

Keleila did her best to follow my directions. "Oh my God, Patrice," she paused. "He looks just like your dad!"

Instantly, the tears began to flow heavily from my eyes. Keleila hugged me, "It's ok." She reassured me, "It's ok." It was surreal. Something out of a dream.

Ms. Williams caught sight of my tears and asked, "Is everything ok?"

"Yea, I just see my uncle in here."

"Here? Did you know he was here?"

"No, not at all. I hadn't seen him in at least fifteen to twenty years. It just caught me by surprise. I looked at the crowd and our eyes instantly locked. I knew then that was definitely him."

"You know you don't have to dance if you don't want to or if it's too emotional."

"No, I'm ok. Can I go first, to get it over with?"

"Absolutely."

Keleila looked at me. "Are you sure?"

"Yea, I'm good. I'll dance." After taking a deep breath, I walked to the center to take my position. The applause settled, waiting for me to start. The music grew slowly. It was a powerful performative piece. The lyrics tell an emotional story, driven with power and passion. I chose this song because of its beautiful musicality and varying melodies. I took the meaning of the song to interpret the longing of a mother's love she has for her lost child, not knowing if he's safe or if he's ok. Maybe her tears will provide a sense of peace, of comfort in seeing each other again one day.

The song ended in a harmonious fade, and I glided off stage. The entire team watched in silence. Returning for a final curtesy, everyone was on their feet, cheering. I made my way to the holding area and broke down, sobbing like a baby. Keleila was right there.

"Patrice, that was incredible!"

One of the security guards saw me crying and asked if I was ok. I explained, "I just saw my uncle and that I had no idea he was here." He asked me his name, and I pointed to him in the crowd.

The guard said, "He's one of the good ones. Never gets into trouble with nobody. Wanna talk to him?"

I was hesitant but a forced "Ok" came out. The guard brought him over and we sat at a table.

Uncle Fred said, "You were really good."

"Thanks."

"How did you know it was me?"

"I saw you wink at me."

"You still look the same. Like the little, big-headed ten-year-old when you used to visit Mama down south." We laughed.

"My friend said that you look just like daddy." And we laughed again. Our impromptu visit ended as the guard told him his time was up.

"I'm doing ok. You take care of yourself. Tell everyone I said hi."

"Ok." And he was led back to the other inmates.

As soon as we got back on campus, I called home. I couldn't wait to tell dad I had just seen his baby brother.

"Hello, Ma, guess what? You know today the dance troupe performed at the East Moline Correctional Facility for Black History Month."

"Oh, Yea. How did it go?"

"Ma, I saw Uncle Fred!!!

Keleila yelled in the background, "Ms. Kuykendal, he looked just like Mr. Kuykendal."

"Ma, I just started crying."

"Oh, I'm sure it was hard seeing him like that."

Keleila shouted from the back "I was there for her, Ms. Kuykendal."

"Tell Keleila that's right, you girls take care of each other. What did he look like?"

"He kind of looked the same. At first, I wasn't sure if it was him, then he winked. That's how I knew for sure it was him. The guard let us talk for a few minutes, and he said I was good at dancing. Is Daddy there?"

"Nah, he's not home. They let you talk to him?

"Yea, it was a medium-security prison. No bars or nothing. They were just sitting on bleachers."

"Really? Did he see you dance?"

"Uh huh, he did. I didn't know how to take it all in?" It was kinda hard seeing him like that, you know? Make sure you tell Daddy, ok?"

"As soon as he gets in."

Daddy called me a couple of hours later. "Hey, your Ma told me you saw Fred today. Did he see you? Know who you were?"

"Yea, they let me talk to him. He looked a little older but pretty much the same. There were about 300 inmates, but I saw him instantly. Like our eyes just connected. He knew me right away, too, because he winked at me. I started crying when I saw him."

"Why were you crying?"

"Why was I crying? I don't know." This was all I could muster.

"Fred, he's alright. He could be better if he stayed his ass out of jail."

"You really think he's alright?"

"He could be worse, but he's probably better off where he is now."

"Ok."

"You need anything?"

"Send me some money."

He pretended to have a bad phone connection. "I'm sorry I can't hear you, baby girl. Must be a bad connection."

"Daddy!!!"

He laughed it off. "Ok, ok, I'll have your Ma put something in the mail. I'll talk to you later."

"Ok, thanks, bye." I hung up the phone.

I pondered the question again, why was I crying? The memories of my uncle were not of him being locked up in a jail cell. They were good times, full of joy and laughter. To see him in this state overwhelmed me. I didn't want to remember him like this, but then again, I had no choice.

THE DECISION

Chapter IX – Hello WIU

My popularity rose within the team during the spring semester. As a result, the team voted me President. I choreographed most of the routines, and I had natural leadership abilities. I was fair, honest, and a hard worker. A new vibe resonated on the yard with the dancers. Almost all the veteran members left, and major crowds were now packing the auditorium for our performances.

During spring auditions, there were a total of twelve guys who tried out. Keleila whispered, "Look at all these guys." Word had gotten out and they wanted to dance. We grew from an eleven-member squad to twenty-five. This team pushed my creativity, and we became really good. I choreographed solos, duets, and large group numbers. I hated the responsibility of costumes, so I made Keleila the costume coordinator. She was in charge of all things costume related. It was a huge undertaking, and she was phenomenal in that role. I was immensely proud.

I wanted my entire family to come to my spring concert, but unfortunately, everyone was busy living their life. Darice was attending Central State University, an HBCU in Ohio, to be close to her NCAA Big Ten scouted basketball-playing boyfriend. Denice was busy growing in the rank of international banking, and Daddy was managing all the rental property, which kept his plate full. However, a mother's love is never far away nor forgotten. Ma took the train and brought Bub to watch my performance. After our concert, the chatter on the yard was the new members gave life back to the dance team, but in reality, the dance team gave all of us life.

I returned to Western the following year. No longer naïve or immature, so I thought. I continued as President of the Dance Troupe but delegated some of the choreographing to the members. As sophomores, we were ecstatic about finally having the needed hours and grade point average to pledge. We often talked about it in secrecy in our dorm room, but that was the extent of it. Keleila and I watched one of our closest friends cross the burning sands. The quiet murmur across campus was a particular group of ladies was finally going to get their chapter reactivated. That was the sorority Keleila and I were most interested in. Unfortunately, they were inactive on the yard and had been for some time due to an unknown incident off-campus.

In jest, Keleila would say threateningly, "You know they're going to make you dance for twelve straight hours." We would laugh just at the thought of being hazed.

Greek life definitely brought some needed excitement to the campus. Community service projects, talent showcases, and step shows were the social highlight. Having a pageant background, I decided to compete in the black and gold pageant. This event was held in the thick of winter by the organization Alpha Phi Alpha Fraternity, Incorporated. They were a group of young men, deemed highly intelligent and socially aware. We loved the Alphas and their consciousness. Besides, Dr. Martin Luther King Jr. was an Alpha man.

I was one of six young ladies competing for the title of Miss Black and Gold. The competition was divided into three sections: Questions & Answers (Q & A), Talent, and Poise. I loved performing, and this gave me another opportunity to dance. My friends couldn't believe I had the nerve to get in front of all those people. However, the more I practiced, the more confident I became. Keleila was my oratory coach. She helped me prepare for the Q &A portion of the pageant.

"Patrice, what if they ask you, 'What's your dream in life?'"

I stood up, shoulders back, chin up, and took a deep breath. "My dream in life is not to directly benefit myself. It's to help others, which in turn is a blessing in being able to help others shine. To discover my purpose in serving mankind. That's my dream in life."

Keleila just looked at me. "You made that up? Wow! That was perfect, Patrice. I hope you get that question."

With her nonstop laughter, she continued. "Ok, let's practice another one. "What has been your biggest accomplishment thus far?"

I took a ceremonious breath and said, "I've been very blessed…"

Keleila interrupted, "Oh yeah, that's good. Throw religion in it. The judges won't give low scores if you mention anything relating to God. Ok, I'm sorry. Go ahead, continue."

"I've been very blessed to receive a college education. I want to continue to make my parents proud and not take this opportunity for granted. While I haven't finished yet, I know that earning my college degree will be one of my biggest accomplishments by showing that hard work and determination can equal success. Thank you." Looking at Keleila, I asked, "How was that? What you think? Cuz, I honestly couldn't think of anything grandiose."

"Patrice, you are doing really well. I don't know how you do it. I'd be a nervous wreck. Hell, I'm not even in the pageant, and I'm already a nervous wreck. You not nervous?"

"Not really. I just need to continue to go over practice questions just to be ready."

"Here's some advice. If you get stuck, just say Dr. Martin Luther King, Jr." "Huh?"

"Trust me; it'll work. Let's try it. Ask me a question."

"Ok, Keleila, if you had one wish, what would that wish be?"

Keleila stood up, looked in the mirror, smiled, and with a straight face, very confidently said, "Dr. Martin Luther King, Jr." I completely lost it and fell to the floor, dying from laughter.

"You see, this way the audience will solely focus on the greatness of Dr. King. No one would ever boo you or give low points just by saying Dr. King's name."

I have to admit her logic was so nonsensical and purely comedy.

"Is Darice and Denice still coming?"

"Yea, they're taking the train down. Get in on Friday."

"Patrice, that's so nice your sisters are supporting you. You do know I'm going to be a nervous wreck, and I'm gonna need their support too?" I laughed at her antics because she was full of drama. I often ignored it because she wholeheartedly meant well.

Keleila confessed. "I might as well be on that stage because I am not going to be able to handle the pressure from the Q & A, so forgive me now because I'm going to politely raise my church finger and exit stage left."

"You're going to leave the room?"

"My anxiety is gonna kick my ass if I don't." Keleila was dead serious. That's how much of a friend she was.

Couldn't bear the thought of her best friend bombing on stage.

"Thanks for the vote of confidence," I teased her. "Trust me; I'm going to do fine, Keleila. I will take a deep breath, exhale, and answer the best way I know how. And if my brain freezes, I now know to say, Dr. Martin Luther King, Jr. Now stop it, before you make me nervous."

Keleila was comedic by default. Not in a pretentious, attention-seeking way but as the youngest of seven siblings, I'm sure she had to scream for attention in her household. She came from a beautiful family of six sisters and one brother. Everyone had either green or hazel eyes. The sisters were all college-educated and drop-dead gorgeous. I remember the first piece of advice they gave us before going away to college was: 1. Don't be roommates, and 2. Don't have sex because that's all boys want. We laughed so hard we fell to the floor. They were an interesting family. I think unusually fascinating would best describe them.

Visiting Keleila, I recall everyone swearing like sailors in their house. The shocking part was that it was in front of their mother, and sometimes, even towards their mother. It was quite a sight to see. I never understood it. As teenagers, an argument in their house would easily turn into a yelling match filled with expletives being shouted at each other. That type of language appeared to be no big deal.

I vividly remember picking up Keleila to head downtown to hang out on Rush Street. I sat in the car, waiting for Keleila to come out. "Bang!" The front door slammed with Keleila screaming, "Dumb Bitches! Fuck You! Fuck all y'all. You crazy motherfuckers!" She skipped down the stairs and hopped into the car. I sat stunned. There's no way I could ever use that type of language and live to tell about it. It was so odd to me because on most days, they were very loving to one another. Besides, culturally speaking, it's rare to witness children speaking to their parents in such a foul, disrespectful manner.

"Those motherfuckers in 6711 are certifiably crazy." I was taken aback.

Then, her mother opened the door, "Don't come back here, you raggedy bitch."

"You crazy old Bitch! Pull off, Patrice." I did what I was told and awkwardly drove off.

"Sorry about all that. I know the Kuykendal household don't have to deal with crazy bat shit like that."

My teenage brain couldn't begin to process what had just happened. I continued toward downtown and Keleila acted as if nothing happened.

On what seemed like the coldest day of the year, Darice and Denice hopped off the Amtrak train, ready to support their youngest sister in the Miss Black and Gold pageant.

"Lawd, it's so freaking cold," Darice mouthed, blowing a puff of white steam into her hands. "Why does it have to be so cold? Jesus!" Darice grabbed her bag from the train car.

"Come on, let's go. It's definitely not getting any warmer complaining about it." Denice threw her hood over her head and picked up her suitcase and waited for Marie's blue escort to pull in the vestibule.

Keleila and I met Marie at Western. She was a year older and originally from Lynwood, Illinois, twenty-five minutes outside of the city. Even though Marie was sweet and quiet, she definitely had a sarcastic wit to her personality. She'd cut you with her slick words when you least expected it. She was also one of the few students lucky enough to have a car on campus.

I had my final rehearsal before the big night, so Marie and Keleila agreed to pick up Darice and Denice from the train station. I met them back in the room afterward.

"Hey, hey, now!" They all screamed when I entered the room. I was ecstatic to see them. With them being here, it meant the world to me.

"Why is it so cold down here?" Darice asked.

Keleila said, "That's all Darice has been talking about."

"No, like for real. This is ridiculous! It's colder here than back home." We just laughed at her assessment.

"You ready for your big day?" Denice asked.

"Yea, I think so," Keleila politely interrupted. "Y'all know Patrice is ready. She stays ready. I've been making sure she practices for the Q & A. I'm more nervous than she is and don't know if I'm going to be able to sit through it."

"Keleila, you're crazy. That doesn't make any sense," Marie said.

"Imma try."

"Girl, please! You'll be sitting in the audience. You not gonna be the one onstage," Marie retorted.

Keleila turned to Denice, "Make sure I don't get up and leave out, ok?"

Grinning, Denice said, "Ok, Keleila, I'll make sure of it."

After several bouts of more laughter, we decided to call it a night in preparations for tomorrow.

Denice made sure I had everything packed and ready to go. "Do you have your costume ironed? Let me steam your gown. Ma would have a fit if we came all the way down here and didn't take care of you."

My nerves were slowly taking charge, but I managed a yes, please, and thank you. Darice decided her talents were better suited cosmetically, so she did my makeup and hair. "How do you want to wear it?"

"Just make it pretty," I said. I sat in the chair as she rolled her sleeves up.

"I'm no magician, but I'll do the best I can with what I have," she said, laughing at her own corny jokes.

"Shut up," I said.

In less than two hours, I would be on my way. "Y'all please don't be late. They say it's going to start at exactly 7:00 pm. No CP time." This was a lie because, as college kids, we didn't do anything on time. I entered the hall and began carving out a small space to serve as a makeshift dressing area. The house of the auditorium began to fill up fast. I peeked from behind the curtain and was able to see my crew out there chatting it up.

We started at 7:30 pm, which wasn't too bad for CP time. Introductions were first, followed by the talent portion, the formal gown, and lastly, the Q & A session. So far, so good because I felt confident about my choreographed dance in the talent competition.

I took the stage for my intro. I mixed it up a bit to combine part Spanish and part English in my opening monologue. I could tell it was well-received by the sound of the applause. After the final round, each contestant remained on stage for the infamous Q & A section.

The announcer called, "Next, we have Miss Patrice Kuykendal." The master of Ceremony was a handsome male in his third year of school. He was quite popular and belonged to the first fraternity established in 1906 for African American Men. He asked, "What is your ultimate goal in life?"

I stepped confidently to the microphone to own the moment. With my smile plastered on my face, I accentuated my long legs in my model stride. I used a well-known pageant trick to help maintain my three-hour smile for the judges. Simply spread Vaseline on your teeth, and this would prevent your jaws from locking or cramping.

I saw a shadowy figure move in the crowd. This figure hurriedly weaved in and out in between the seats, trying to dimly excuse themselves. *"Oh Gosh."* It was my dear friend Keleila. She desperately tried to remain still, but her self-imposed anxiety couldn't afford her the tranquility to sit through this part of the presentation. Granted, she did forewarn me. In a flash, right before my eyes, Keleila made a beeline toward the illuminated exit sign. She was out the door. I knew she meant well, but she just couldn't contain her emotionally charged passion or be able to process if her bestie bombed on stage in front of all those people. It might as well have been her on the stage that day. It was too much for her to deal with, even if it was all in her head. If you're lucky enough, God gives you one true friend, and I was fortunate to have her in my corner.

I gathered my composure, quickly collected my thoughts, and framed my words to perfect my sentence, "My ultimate goal in life is to..." My mind drew a blank, and I thought of Keleila's go-to answer, reciting Dr. Martin Luther King Jr. The room went dark, and I became motionless. Was the room spinning? Everything froze. All I could see was Keleila abandoning me—that moment flashed before my eyes. All I could remember was the MC repeating his question in a slow-motion haze. My vision blurred the lines of my thoughts, but finally, I came through. "My ultimate goal in life is to help others. To discover my purpose in serving all mankind, and by doing so, I hope to leave this world a better place. Thank you." I admit it was very pageant(esque), maybe even borderline cheesy. But hey, by any means necessary, and I had come to win.

Keleila quietly tipped back to her seat. I was relieved, the hardest part was finally over for her. I meant over for me. All contestants reentered the auditorium and took their respective spots on stage. They announced the winners. I came in first runner up, which was unacceptable for me. I surmised it was because the winner was Greek and an upperclassman. This is called rationalizing your loss. It was a fun experience though. Not long after that, a few sororities actively pursued my membership, which was interesting in itself. Hilarious how my identity on the yard expanded to being known as *"Patrice the dancer."*

The ushering of spring melted the final mounds of packed snow. Being so close to Chicago, we definitely had to deal with our share of the brutal winter. And for the record, you never get used to it. You just deal with it. The warmer weather lightened everyone's mood. The college parties became plentiful as we peeled off the extra layers of clothes. It was a fair trade of red cup libations. I barely dated in college, and it was practically nonexistent in high school, and that's putting it mildly. I was 'strictly dickly' and never got into that girl-on-girl college experimentation people speak about in college.

I did date one nice guy in college. Honestly, it didn't feel much like dating, though. It felt like a true friendship relationship. Which isn't how a relationship is supposed to feel? Malachi was one of the nicest guys I've ever met. However, it wasn't romantic at all. There was no sex or deep-throated kisses. We hung out and enjoyed each other's company, laughing a lot. Frankly, it felt kind of weird when he would attempt to kiss me and try his hand at romanticism. One time, I blurted, "What are you doing?" He didn't answer and took it as a slight rejection. I adored his personality, but I wasn't attracted passionately to him. On a few occasions, Malachi found himself trapped in our room after visiting curfew hours. We had to get him out unsuspectingly before our nightly room check by our resident assistant.

Naturally, two girls from the southside of Chicago schemed a hilarious

plan. Keleila said, "Malachi, if you get busted, tell that fat bitch, Julie, you were visiting the white chicks in room 730."

I told Malachi, "No, we gotta sneak you out before she does her rounds."

"I'll just walk out to the elevator," Malachi said.

In unison, Keleila and I both squealed, "No!" We already received a warning a week ago for a noise violation, and one more infraction would get us a formal write-up. We couldn't take that chance. Keleila came up with an idea that only *she* could think of. "Malachi, we'll dress you up like a girl. This way, she wouldn't know the difference." I couldn't stop laughing, but if he was willing to try it, it might just work.

Keleila handed Malachi a long red house robe. Being six feet-three inches, the sleeves were ultra-short on him, and he looked like the wolf in Little Red Riding Hood. "Don't kill me, but you gotta cover your head with a scarf or something." He complained because we couldn't stop laughing at how funny he looked. Keleila tried to get serious. "Malachi, all kidding aside. We can't get written up again. Please, Malachi, just try it. You can take all this off when you get on the elevator because, in the mighty words of Dr. Martin Luther King, Jr., 'You'll be free at last.'"

We laughed for another five minutes. He allowed us to continue to play dress-up with him, and I handed him a red bandana. "Tie this on your head and keep your head down when you're walking, ok?"

Keleila piped in, "Show us how you're gonna walk." Being the nice guy that he was, he obliged. Malachi motioned a walk as if he was female. Now he was entertaining us. I literally fell off the bed from laughing so hard. "No, Malachi, you gotta move like this," Keleila said shuffling her feet with her head held down low. "Don't take this the wrong way, but right now, you look like the abolitionist Sojourner Truth." We were now rolling with laughter on the cramped dorm room floor.

Malachi snatched the scarf off his head. "Nope, I'm not doing it." This had to be the funniest night in college history. We finally stopped laughing and convinced him to go through with it. Malachi agreed by saying, "Y'all better not tell anybody about this either."

"Ok, we promise. Call us when you get back to your room." We peeked in the halls to make sure it was clear and empty. We pushed Malachi out the door with crossed fingers, praying that we wouldn't get caught.

Malachi was an amazing person, but we didn't date very long. It was such an authentic friendship, I figured we'd always be in each other's lives, but unfortunately, that wasn't the case. Spring fling was real, and I'm not solely talking about the weather. On the yard, I met a guy named Dre. He was tall, and by all accounts, a bad boy with a thugga-thug vibe. He had that *"I don't give a fuck attitude"* in his walk. He was intriguing and the total opposite of Malachi. One day, I caught him looking at me in the café. I quickly looked away. He would always make small talk, but that was about it. While I admired his looks from afar, we never got together, despite what Malachi suspected. Yes, he was intriguing, but that was the extent of it.

Honestly, I grew bored with Malachi and was 100 percent honest when he confronted me as I was leaving the café.

"Hey, wait up."

I could feel his energy when I responded, "What's up?" We continued walking. What used to be a casual natural stroll was now tense and strangely uncomfortable. I broke the ice with mundane gossip. "You see Marie on line? She looks scared shit-less. She left a note in my mailbox with her car keys. I had to get her a..."

He interrupted me. "P, you seeing Dre?" I stopped in my tracks.

"Dre?" I grew defensive. *So, what if I am! We're not married, Malachi! You know, he's everything you're not. He's confident and cool. Don't get me wrong, you're nice, but you're boring as fuck. Oh yeah, and news flash, he thinks I'm sexy, and I forgot to mention, when he looks at me it's lustful and wanting!"*

"P! P?"

I heard Malachi calling my name in the distance, which made me snap out of my daydream. I could have never said those hurtful things to him. Instead, I opted for "No, Malachi, I'm not." There was no need to destroy a person's spirit. I didn't want to break him. Besides, he didn't deserve that, and it was the God's honest truth.

I spoke to Dre a couple of times on the phone and quickly realized some guys needed to be left right where they are...on the yard. However, it was too late, the rumor mill had spun, and Malachi chose to believe it. I didn't even try to convince him otherwise.

Marie finally crossed the burning sands and was now an official sorority girl. It was a lifelong dream of hers, and I was proud of her achievement. My good friend, Michael, also crossed into his fraternity. Which I thought was an odd choice for his personality. Their probate shows were a jubilant moment for the entire campus. We cheered and showered them with gifts for accomplishing this major milestone. I was so proud of them.

Not surprisingly, I bumped into Malachi with very few words spoken. He played the victimization card. I let him and ignored his sulking and silent treatment toward me. The end of the school year activities were wrapping up, and campus was slowly becoming desolate. Everyone was packing for the summer, exchanging numbers, and saying their goodbyes.

THE DETERMINATION

Chapter X — Summer's Here

Daddy and Bub came down to drive me back for the summer break. I swear, where did I accumulate so much stuff. I was cramped in the back seat but grateful to get to my own room with my own bed. I figured I'd look for a summer job when I got home. I've always worked part-time to have my own money, and I would take dance classes somewhere. I was looking forward to being home for the next three months. I found summer work at a factory bottling carefree jheri curl products. I hated the smell, but I didn't care because I would be making my own money. At work, we had to wear all white with a white hair net and steel toe shoes that weighed at least ten pounds.

My first day on the job, I was paired with a group of veterans, affectionately called the old-timers. They had been with the company for twenty-five-plus years and were nearing the golden years of retirement. They were a hoot with a sweet spirit. Aside from looking like nurses in our uniform, I never quite understood the steel-toe shoes. Did they anticipate a fifty-pound weight dropping on our feet or something? I sucked it up and checked my personal style at the punch clock. The carefree curl activator smell was repugnant, offensive, and it lingered in your pores endlessly.

A woman named Betty was assigned to mentor me on my shift. She asked, "Have you heard of the Saran Wrap?" Betty belonged to the old-timer's crew. Her silver hair was kept in a bun under her shower cap. Her face barely graced any lines of maturity, and I could still detect a warm southern drawl in some of her words.

I replied, "Saran, Ms. Betty?"

"Yeah, the plastic, Saran wrap?"

I asked, "What would I use that for?"

"You're so slim; I guess you don't need that stuff, huh?" She said with a hearty laugh. I honestly had no idea what she's referring to. "What do you do with it?"

"You'll see soon enough. Everybody wraps up when they get in so they can use the company's plastic."

The next morning, I punched in and quickly centered myself at the end of the conveyor belt, opposite from Betty. This was where all the new people started. It was a messy and fast assembly line. Being at the end gave you an advantage for the upkeep of the bottles. This allowed extra time to prepare and set up until you got used to it.

One of the old-timers yelled out with a husky chuckle, "Hey, youngin! You ready?" He thought I didn't hear him when he whispered, "This 'bout to be funny as hell." But I heard his old ass. Trying not to seem too nervous, I gave him the thumbs-up signal to start the damn belt. The thunderous roar and cranking of the machine had a deafening sound which made everyone scream from the top of their voices when they talked to each other. My heart began to palpitate as the machine got noisier and louder.

Betty shouted, "Sweetie start lining up your bottles; here they come."

Quickly, I reached into my supply and pulled out five empty bottles.

"Hurry."

It was my job to assemble the bottles precisely under the spouts that contained the product. I had to cap and wipe the bottle down before packaging them for shipment, which wouldn't have been so difficult if you actually had time to lock and load the bottles properly on the belt before they started moving. Perspiration was popping off my forehead and sweat had seeped right through the pit of my underarms, leaving the biggest sweat stains on my uniform. It was a fast-paced job, but I got the hang of it and somehow managed to pack my first five bottles without mishap.

"Youngin, that was a test, but we can't continue to work at that pace, or boss will come out here and fire us all." He cranked the speed of the machine.

Betty said, "Pay him no mind. He teases all the pretty young summer students. Go ahead and get those bottles ready; here they come. Just concentrate on what you're doing. You'll get it soon enough."

The belt was moving far too fast for me to keep up. As soon as one row preceded, I was already reaching and grabbing five more. Then suddenly, a spout clogged. In desperation, I tried to snatch and remove two bottles, only to knock over the third one. I tried resetting them on the belt, but to no avail. The activator gushed and spilled on the apparatus and all over the floor. The gel-like substance was white and cloudy-looking. It oozed from the machines, dripping all over the bottles, even onto my lovely steel toe shoes. The smell was atrocious!

"Hit the button!" a voice shouted. "Halt the damn machine!" A ball-fisted hand slammed and punched the red nuclear button to power off the entire system. Embarrassed, I stood frozen, looking at the contraption that single-handily ruined my total existence.

A voice announced on the intercom, "Fifteen-minute break, people. We got a mess to clean."

I retreated to the locker room. I wiped my shoes and tried to piece my dignity back together. I sat there thinking, only seven more hours to go. Betty approached me.

"You hang in there, youngin. Most college kids hardly last a day. Shoot, that little accident was nothing. Just don't quit. Keep showing up. You'll get the hang of it. We all been where you are. Pull that chin up, missy. You hear me?"

I felt like a failure. But I needed a summer job, and here I was. "Thank you, Ms. Betty." I appreciated the break. Standing on your feet all day is no easy feat, but somehow Ms. Betty definitely made it all a little more worthwhile.

"Ms. Betty, what are those ladies doing?" I asked.

"Remember, the Saran? She's helping her to wrap it around her body. Look around, over there..." She pointed to two ladies; the first had her shirt raised, while the other was circling her body with clear cellophane.

"Make it tighter," the lady screamed. The lady engulfed her stomach to squeeze in five rotations.

"But why?"

Betty pointed to a trio near the stalls and explained they were doing what is called "a doubling." On heavier people, they use two people to double the wraps, constricting any excess flab with two rotating in the opposite direction. Betty fixed her hairnet and asked, "You never heard or seen that before, have you? The plastic traps in the body heat, and it makes you sweat and lose weight. The pounds just melt off, and you can still eat whatever you want. All the women here wrap up. Even some men too. They try to keep it on their entire eight-hour shift and then unwrap when it's time to go home. We all wrap up, see?" She pulled back her blouse to let the plastic peek through.

I thought, *"Well, with steel toe shoes, protective goggles, hair nets, curl activator, and now, a do-it-yourself plastic diet kit, this is going to be an arduous summer."*

A letter from my university came addressed to my parents. I had no idea they were my grades. I finished last semester with a modest 2.7 GPA. Nothing to brag about, but hey, at least, I hadn't flunked out. School was mediocre. There was nothing exceptional about it. I still didn't have any idea of career goals, declaring a major or even a minor. My parents had a cavalier attitude toward education. It was an unspoken expectation. There was never pressure to do this or to do that. There was more or less an unwritten rule, that eventually you'll figure it out because you must do something upon graduation. I was stuck trying to decide what that something was for me. Sure, I enjoyed performing, and I was extremely good at dancing. However, I considered it my professional hobby and not a chosen career path.

When daddy mentioned my grades, I spun the conversation this way— "Daddy, I almost got a 3.0, which is close to a B average."

My father looked at me and smirked. "I know what a B average is....and 2.7 is not a 3.0."

I brushed it off.

"I know, I know, I almost said." I ended with, "Imma do better." And that was the extent of it. I assumed they trusted me enough to know that I would eventually, hopefully, and prayerfully find my way and figure it out. Luckily, they gave me time to discover and develop my passions without any pressure, stress, or anxiety, and for that, I was completely grateful.

I couldn't wait to continue my dance lessons. I outgrew my adolescent studio and set my sights on professional companies that offered classes. I knew the environment would be more challenging, but it would take my skill set to the next level. Something I desperately craved.

In college, I recalled seeing the Joseph Holmes Dance Company perform "Mary, Don't You Weep." It was breathtaking, spiritual storytelling at its best. The piece was choreographed to Aretha Franklin's rendition of the gospel song. The movement was ethereal, grounded in the African American tradition of finding hope in an otherwise hopeless time.

Under the artistic direction of Randy Duncan, Joseph Holmes was a premiere dance company with founding roots in Chicago. I located the company and signed up to take ballet, jazz, and modern. It was a professional atmosphere with an audition board between the gender-identified locker rooms. It was tightly managed with hundreds of bodies coming and going through the doors of its former art district location.

While I tended to be somewhat aloof personally, the dance community was one of love, acceptance, and always very welcoming. I loved that about this free artistic expression. In an industry where you're judged on performance, looks, technique, and overall talent, I always felt the least judged in this inclusive setting. Dancers just want to dance. That's it, and that's all. I studied the audition board intently. I had no clue what I was doing, but I decided to do more than just stare at the postings. I started writing them down. Every week, I would look. Every week I would copy at least two down. I didn't have the courage or confidence to actually attend any of these auditions yet, but it inspired me and gave me hope of what could exist.

I continued to work at the factory and found solace in dance. I ventured up north to Evanston a few times to study with Gus Giordano, but the commute was outreaching. I appreciate all styles of dance. However, there was something uniquely magical in the lines of the African American experience and tradition. Maybe it was how our ancestors used negro spirituals as a testimony of their survival and faith. Since we had been culturally deprived and alienated from our families, language, and culture, we used our creativity as a tool of communication. They took stories from the bible and created their own folklore. For me, the reckoning of our culture was profoundly rooted in greatness. I felt this in every ounce of the word.

Searching the white pages of the phone book, I came across the Boulevard Arts Center, located on 55th street. I called and was told I could take a class for ten dollars. It was a straight path from my house, so I decided to see what they had to offer. The class was located in the basement of a parochial school building. When I arrived, there were three people at the barre, and the teacher stood in the corner. He was a tiny, frail man with a solemn expression.

"Hi, I'm here for class. It's my first time. The lady on the phone said it was ten dollars."

The teacher took the money and said, "Hurry and change. The restroom is on the right."

There wasn't much light since we were in the basement, and it was a tight space, more like a closet. I slipped out of my clothes to reveal my basic leotard and tights. I followed the others and took a position at the barre.

"Let's get started," the instructor announced. "I'm Tommy, and we will incorporate Graham with the Dunham technique."

I began to notice that professional companies focused on techniques and styles. These names were becoming more familiar in describing dance technique: Horton, Fosse, Graham, Dunham, as in Katherine Dunham. It was a lot to learn. This place trained dancers using Ms. Dunham's style. Like a sponge, I soaked it all in—every company, every style, every studio, and every technique. I was loving my eclectic dance journey.

The instructor motioned me to come away from the bar. I quickly fell in line. I was the only girl, and the other three guys appeared somewhat older. "Have you studied dance before?" he asked.

"Yes."

"Then you will have no problem catching up. Move to the middle."

I adjusted my position. I could tell the other dancers knew Tommy really well. He was hard on them and demanded perfection of their body. As a new student, he afforded me a two-week grace period, and then the bar was raised. He had high expectations of all of us in that basement. I did my best to keep up. My kicks slowly became higher. My stamina improved, and I was able to hold my extensions with more core control.

It wasn't until much later that I realized I was training under the former principal dancer, Tommy Gomez of the late great Katherine Dunham's company. My confidence grew, and I was constantly checking the weekly audition listings. One day after class, I exchanged niceties with a fellow dancer, named Keith. It felt like innocent flirtation. Or maybe it was my intimate imagination. I mean, sweating in tights and body stockings provides the ample opportunity of envisioning everything, and I do mean E.V.E.R.Y.T.H.I.N.G. At times, I found myself silently staring at Keith, taking him all in. His skin was smooth, like chocolate. His body was lean and muscular. Keith's six-foot-two-inch frame was long with chiseled abs. He looked like he was straight out of an Ailey repertoire. Do I need to say that he was easy on the eyes? He was. I felt energized in his presence.

"Patrice, Patrice?" Keith snapped me out of my trance.

"Uh, huh?"

"I thought I lost you for a moment. Do you ever audition?"

"Nah, I'm still building my nerves up, but I do check the audition board."

"You should. You're really good, and I can tell Tommy thinks so too. There's so much happening here…shows, musicals, movies, and they're all looking for dancers. Beautiful dancers such as yourself."

"Thank you," I said sheepishly. "I've been checking some of the listings, but I haven't gone on any. I see some postings, but I'm trying to raise my game first."

"You should. You're pretty good, and you have the look. Sometimes that's all it takes."

"Really?"

"There's one coming up, and they're looking for tall, pretty female dancers. You should go." Keith wrote down the information and handed it to me. "Oh, and that's my number on the other side." I laughed and grinned. He smiled too.

"Ok, thanks. I will think about it." *He was definitely flirting.*

"Which one? The audition or calling me?"

As I walked away, I yelled, "Both!" and shrugged my shoulders. I gazed back. He was still staring at me. I let his words set in, *"You have the look. You're pretty good." "Maybe I should go,"* I thought to myself. What's the worst thing that could happen? I was on cloud nine.

THE DETERMINATION

Chapter XI – Goodbye WIU

I read the casting notice again. Tall, pretty females with extensive dance training. ALL STYLES written in caps. Bring character and ballet shoes, 4:00 pm sharp. Industrial musical, excellent pay. I threw caution to the wind and decided to go. I didn't have character shoes, just ballet slippers. I packed my bag and went directly from work. It was the only thing I could focus on all day. I was going to my first dance audition. My heart was smiling on the inside.

Immediately after work, I found the address pretty easily. It was downtown. After checking the time, I rushed inside to the fourth floor. It was already 4:05 pm, and I hated being late. I hadn't anticipated traffic and made it right before all the audition numbers were exhausted.

A voice called, "Please step up and sign-in if you haven't done so and make sure your number is visible."

"Hi, I need to register."

The lady handed me a form with a pen. It asked for detailed information, name, weight, availability, clothing size, waist, and hip measurements. None of which I knew. I left most of them blank and entered the most important stuff like name, phone number, and address. I handed my form to the lady at the desk.

She looked at my blank spaces, then asked, "Do you have a headshot?"

I glanced and saw most girls holding their form with a gigantic 8 x 10 picture attached. "No, I don't."

"Step over here."

I barely made it inside the box before she snapped my picture with a polaroid camera. The flash was blinding. She stapled it to my paper and handed me a huge number that read seventy-eight. Was I the seventy-eighth girl here? I glanced down at the audition notice and completely shrank. In boldface type, it read, "Industrial Production at the Arie Crown Theater, $600 pay plus $400 for two days of rehearsal. Ten ladies with two swing dancers." There had to be at least 100 dancers here easily. And ten ladies, I thought, *You've got to be kidding me!*

Gorgeous bodies were everywhere, sprawled in every nook and corner in an attempt to grab a piece of space to stretch and warm their bodies. Legs graced the air, practicing battements and extensions. Others chose to reveal major skin to showcase their sex appeal. Powder makeup was being passed around, and lips were painted red. Body acceptance was not yet a thing, so pretty much all the girls looked the same. Tall, white, skinny, repeat. I've always been considered a slim girl, but genetically, I felt more skinny-thick, or so I'd like to think.

My self-esteem was plummeting by the minute. If I entered the room on a confidence scale of ten, it was probably a three at this point. A voice popped in my head, *"You better stay and do this, girl. Don't you dare even consider it."* I thought, "Me, consider what?" Taking my measly confident three and bolting straight out the door. My inner thoughts were getting the best of me, and self-doubt was winning. I wanted to disappear and escape this self-imposed madness. I tried to get out of my head. I took a deep breath and ultimately decided to stay.

I pulled my sweats over my tights and leotard. I looked at myself in the mirror and checked my attire. Senselessly, I compared my look to every dancer in the room that day. Noticeably, the dancer standing next to me looked like a vixen. She owned her space. I, on the other hand, looked like I was dressed to take class. One of us clearly didn't get the memo, and I think we know who that was. My self-esteem was now a measly two. If it goes any lower, that's it. I promise, I'm jetting north, straight out the door.

I quickly snatched a small area and began stretching. I tried to focus and not allow the other dancers to distract me. I was consumed with shoulder rolls, neck circles, rib cage releases, and hip flexors for the next five minutes.

A lady stepped up and announced, "Thank you for being here. Wow! There are a lot of you. Shannon? Is that you? What are you doing here, girl?" I tilted my head to look across the room.

"Just got back from LA last night." Shannon said.

"How was LA?"

"Freaking Incredible!"

The lady continued, "I see a lot of new faces and some familiar ones. This gig only calls for ten female dancers and two swing dancers."

What is a swing dancer? I wondered. I had no idea.

"This is a well-paying industrial production with a major client." Cheers and applause interrupted her speech. "So, naturally, we are looking for All-American types—ladies who are upbeat, perky, and personable that can represent the brand. Before we get started, are there any questions?" No one spoke. "Ok, then we will start with a ballet combination, and from there, cuts will be made for the second round. If you make it to round two, you will learn a jazz piece followed by more cuts. Going once, going twice, any questions?"

Shannon raised her hand. "Is it ok if we use pointe shoes for the ballet segment?"

"There's always an over-achiever, right?" the lady said with a smile. The crowd chuckled at her humorless wise-crack. "Sure, Shannon. Go for it."

I thought, *"Shut the hell up, Shannon. Trust, everybody knows you. We know you already have one of the slots on lock."* Slowly, I sucked my teeth and exhaled the negative energy that was consuming my body. The ballet combination was challenging. I knew most of the choreography but struggled with some parts of it. I didn't execute the routine at optimal level, and it was exposed in my performance. I stayed, pushed through, and tried my best. I did not allow fear to win! While I didn't get the audition, I learned an awful lot about myself. It was very humbling. It made me want to expand my training and get out there more. I wasn't about to quit on myself. I had room to grow, and now was the time.

I watched intently as the others auditioned. Some were damn near perfect and flawless in their style. It was captivating to see. I took copious mental notes. Holding my breath, I crossed my fingers and secretly prayed to the dance Gods. My number was not called. I dropped my head. I did not advance to round two.

On my way home, I had to dig awfully deep. I left feeling pretty crushed. It was my first audition, and I BOMBED! It's understandable, how regardless of talent, it's so easy for dancers to give up and get a job in banking.

My first audition made me realize that a thick skin is needed for this industry, and oh, the rejection! You gotta get used to it. But do you ever get used to it? It was tough both mentally and physically. If I wanted any chance of success, I had to get out of my own way. I continued my training while working through summer. Ironically, one gave me life, and the other sucked the life out of me.

When I made it home Ma asked, "How did it go?"

Begrudgingly, I answered, "I didn't get it."

"Oh, well. Get my purse. I need you to go to the store for me."

"Ughhhh, Ma! Don't you wanna hear how it went?"

"No, not at the moment. I wanna hear you going to the store. Hold on, these kids... I tell you." She put the phone down and grabbed her list. "Get a can of pet milk, eggs, and my lotteries. Make sure you open the carton and check the eggs."

"But we don't have a pet?" She glared at me. "Ok, ok, write your numbers down." I said.

I've been buying my parents lottery tickets since I was sixteen. I wasn't old enough, but that didn't stop Jimmy the Greek from selling them to me. He owned the liquor store on the corner. There weren't many liquor stores in the neighborhood at that time, but the street activists were doing their damnedest to shut him down anyway.

He always donated to our annual block club party, which made it kind of hard not to like him.

Ma always held an active position on the block club. This year she was the secretary, but she was revered like the president. She was very involved, and the block loved her. She connected with everyone she met. She would welcome you inside our home and offer you either food, one of her daughters, or some homemade wine. She was always busy, especially with four kids and a patriarch husband. Nonetheless, she would still make time for you. Her warmth and kindness were contagious, and she seldom complained. As the taskmaster queen, she managed the Kuykendal household in tutoring, coaching, cooking, counseling, cleaning, and nursing. It was second nature to her.

As much as I thrust my dad onto a pedestal, I'm sure he wouldn't get the husband of the year award. I'm certain he was probably emotionally unavailable at times. I think Ma just tolerated it. Ma and Daddy married in 1965 when they were barely young adults. Inspired by the post-industrialization era, they moved from their small hometown of Batesville, Mississippi, and headed North to Chicago by way of Detroit. Interestingly, each of their four children had been born in a different state.

I vividly recall the courtship story Ma reminisced about daddy. She never called him by his sir name; it was always Sonny. *"You know, I remember the mosquitoes were biting really bad one summer, and Sonny, you remember what you said to me?"*

Looking unbothered with a half-smirk, Daddy replied, "Nope." I'm sure he remembered but shielding himself from an embarrassing moment, he retreated. We all wanted to hear the story and gathered closer.

"Your father said if you get bitten by one more mosquito, he was going to catch and beat up all those mosquitoes." We laughed. Daddy couldn't help it, so he laughed too—probably at the sheer ridiculousness of the statement. Nevertheless, it was a cute and endearing flashback, revealing a softer, loving side between the two of them.

I returned from the store and took a seat at the kitchen table. "Ma?" She was cooking and didn't stop. I tried again. "Ma?" I think this is one of the most annoying things you can do to a parent. Call their name over, over, and over until they respond. She kept moving from stove to refrigerator to counter to table.

She said, "Open that pet milk for me."

I called out again. "Ma!"

"Girl, I hear you."

"But you didn't say nothing."

She stopped. "Go ahead; I'm listening. Tell me what happened at the audition" "There were 100 or so girls there, and they were only looking for ten. Only ten out of all those girls. Can you believe that? They taught us a ballet combination and then called us out in groups of ten. The piece wasn't that hard."

"Then why you think you didn't get it?"

"I dunno. No, that's not true. Those girls looked professional, and I just looked, well, very plain, boring like an amateur."

"Just go to the next one and the next one and keep going until you're no longer an amateur."

"But what if they're all like that?"

Ma stopped moving and looked at me. "You'll eventually get it. You know how I know? Because you are constantly getting better and growing. Watch and see baby girl. Imma tell you what I know."

That was one of Ma's favorite catchphrases. Which summed up, baby girl, trust me, I do know what I'm talking about. Ma always had a way of turning a negative situation into a positive one.

I actually thought about calling Keith. I decided against it because I didn't feel like rehashing the audition. I knew I would see him soon enough in class, and I would address it then, if it came up. Dating was a misnomer in my world. My focus remained on dance, work, and school. Pretty much in that order.

I decided to continue class in the basement with Tommy. I hadn't been in a serious ballet class for a while, so I decided to return to my ballet roots for added strength and technique. Ballet was my solid base, but it was also important to continue to diversify my training. This led me to discover Joel Hall in the Edgewater neighborhood on the Northside. It was true, there were more artistic opportunities on the north side than the south side of the city. Joel was a cultural icon in the dance world. The artistic director of The Joel Hall Dancers, a multicultural dance company, was committed to the uplift of the African American movement. I frequented his studio for occasional classes and met some wonderful dancers along the way.

Another genius on the scene was a newcomer, ballet phenom, Homer Bryant, former principal dancer with Dance Theater of Harlem. Unfortunately, I never had the honor of studying with Mr. Bryant due to my grueling schedule, but his name was growing in the dance world. One day on my way to a modeling audition, I traveled to the west side of the city. Upon entering the huge dome off Madison street, the sound of Roberta Flack filled the halls. *"The First Time Ever I Saw Your Face"* was sweet and melodic. My ears led me straight to the open gymnasium. I stood in the door and watched as this couple performed a pas de deux. It was breathtaking to watch. An older gentleman barked orders at the two, and I thought he must be the choreographer.

I stood silently for a while and finally interrupted, "Excuse me? Do you know where the fashion show tryouts are?"

The older gentleman said, "At the end of the opposite hall on the fourth floor."

Embarrassed that I disturbed their concentration, I politely said, "Thank you." In that moment, I was transfixed on their movement and stood there for another ten minutes, almost forgetting about my intended audition. Before leaving, I asked, "Do you teach dance here? That piece by Roberta Flack moved my soul."

"Yes, I do. On Tuesdays and Thursdays, 7:00 pm–9:00 pm. Are you a dancer? I'm always looking for more dancers."

I thought to myself, *"Am I a dancer?"* "Yes! I am." The older man's name was Bob Richardson. He looked to be in his mid-60s. I inquired but never learned much history on Bob, except he may have danced with Ailey back in the day. He was tall with a few extra pounds, but I could imagine him in his prime. I mean, his choreography flowed like an emotionally complex love story. I stayed for a few more minutes before leaving for the modeling audition.

Bob said, "Come dance with us, Tuesdays/Thursdays at 7:00 pm."

"I think I will, thanks." I ran upstairs but couldn't stop thinking about the movement I just experienced. Who would have thought that such beautiful dance was tucked away on the westside of Chicago, hidden from the rest of the world?

The fashion show audition was held by a husband-and-wife team. A beautiful couple, I'm assuming, who met through modeling jobs. They decided to form their own company and were in search of beautiful models who could work the runway. Their company was called Fashion Chicago, and they had all these shows lined up throughout the city. They were paid gigs, but you had to commit to Sunday rehearsals. They loved my look and the way I walked. I had a mean walk and could command a room. They wanted to book me for their upcoming shows.

My summer schedule was becoming quite full. I was taking classes and meeting dancers all over the city. My technique was improving, and I was determined to acquaint myself with a variety of Chicago-based choreographers. My first audition was a horrible, an embarrassing experience. Yet, I knew the only way I was going to get better was to continue to put myself out there. Yes, it was scary and frightening, but I continued to audition for any and everything posted. I had to get comfortable in being uncomfortable. I just kept trying, falling down (yes, sometimes literally), only to get back up. I did not get chosen for one dance gig that entire summer, but that didn't stop me from trying. Even gigs that I considered out of my league, I didn't care I showed up. If there was an open call, yours truly was there. I was in growth mode, and finally I started getting callbacks. My auditioning was at least improving, which was a step in the right direction.

I went on so many auditions that summer, I started recognizing familiar faces. I traveled to the west side and added Tuesdays and Thursdays to my already full schedule. Immediately, Bob paired me with this amazing dancer named Greg. We complemented each other physically and technically, and Bob wasted no time teaching me choreography. Before you knew it, Greg was flinging me in the air and seducing me as his lover in this choreographed romantic piece. I have to admit, dancing with a partner was new and exciting, not to mention challenging. I had to learn to trust Greg when he tossed me in the air.

Artistically, Bob taught me the illusion of an emotion I had not yet fully experienced. One of love. Whether it was a subtle look into your partner's eyes or a swaying of the hips, his choreography told a painfully beautiful story of passion.

The summer season was moving fast as it always does. It was one of my favorite seasons next to fall, but we rarely got to experience the enchantment of the leaves changing. I began to question if I wanted to return to Western. I pondered, *"Do I really want to go back?"* I was feeling more purposeful with everything I had going on at home. Aside from my summer job, I was now focused on modeling and dancing at the dome. Don't get me wrong, as a student, I made it work at Western, but I never felt directionally driven. It was almost like, "Yeah, I'm in college, but I don't really know what I want to do with my life." I didn't say a word to anyone about these perplexed feelings. Also, I wasn't sure how they'd respond to this idea. I knew I wanted more, and Western just wasn't giving it to me.

It was mid-July, and I was sitting at our dining room table. I blurted out, "Ma, I'm not going back to Western." I paused and waited for a response.

"Why not?"

"I think I want to do something else."

"Your grades? You not pregnant?"

I'm thinking, pregnant? Like the virgin Mary? "Nooooooo, Ma, I'm not!!! God!!!! My grades were decent." She went back to doing what she was doing.

"Ma?"

"Yeah."

"Trust me, I'm gonna finish college. I need to first figure out what I want to do with my life."

Unmoved, Ma said, "It'll come to you." And just like that, the trajectory of my life changed. I broke the news to my father, making sure I added that I'm going to finish college. Daddy wasn't the least bit worried.

While one weight lifted off my shoulder, another one appeared. Now I had to decide my next plan of action. I hated working at the factory but loved dancing. I tried to release any unnecessary stress, deadlines, or time constraints on my future goals. I would stay open to the possibilities of everything in the universe being available to me. As lofty as these goals were, my personality thrived on absolute and concrete ideals.

My mom was impressed with Fashion Chicago and loved watching me model. Secretly, she would often say, "I want you to model. You're so good at it." I enjoyed modeling, though I never saw myself as supermodel-material. Sure, there was Beverly Johnson, Victoria Webb, Roshumba Williams, Naomi Campbell, and Tyra Banks, but Black models were a novelty and often still discriminated against by the major fashion houses. That industry was too superficial for me. Besides, the business of modeling only allowed a few select Black models to enter while a herd of thousands of skinny white girls received privilege passes. This was why modeling never appealed to me or fully resonated in my spirit. I just didn't see it as a full-time career. Honestly, dance didn't either, but I enjoyed it much more and continued to do both earnestly.

Modeling in my first show with Fashion Chicago went really well. It was fun, super easy, beautiful, and sexy. I exuded a confidence that was undeniable and was chosen for more gigs. We were paid cash for each show and promptly booked for future ones. My parents had no complaints regarding the direction of my life. In hindsight, I wonder if they trusted my instincts and felt that ultimately, I would make decisions that would prove productive and fruitful. It was a beautiful thing to be allowed to grow and become whatever I was going to be.

I remember watching TV and dissecting what was happening within the frame. I became intrigued with working in television and began to research careers in media. Television production piqued my curiosity, and I wanted to discover more. I had no clue where to begin. And just like always, I researched and read everything I could to become more familiar with the subject. At that very moment, it crystalized for me. I will have a career in television production.

I ran to Ma's room, excited, and told her, "I'm going to work behind the scenes in television."

"You should be in front of the camera, don't you think?" Parents are hella funny. They really do think all their children are strikingly beautiful.

"No, I want to work in production, helping to produce the show, putting it together. Behind the camera, not in front." I stumbled upon Columbia College in Chicago. They were known as a liberal arts institution. I signed up for an orientation and quickly decided this was going to be my college of choice.

"Ma and Daddy, I've been reading about Columbia College downtown, and they have a program in television production."

Dad asked, "How much is this going to cost?"

"Not sure yet, but I know I'll get some financial aid to help cover it." He gave a grin of approval. Despite transferring schools in my junior year, I was determined to graduate in four years. I wasn't going to allow anything to stop me from reaching my goal. I started ordering transcripts and meeting with college and financial aid advisors. I learned to quickly advocate for myself when an admission specialist refused to accept some of my academic credits. I politely handed him the course catalog, which was my documentation on why the class was synonymous with one listed on my transcript. I provided evidence, and as a result, Columbia accepted all of my transferred academic credits.

I was on a quest to graduate from college in four years and I had already completed two. I mapped my plan. I created a tracking system of every course required to earn my bachelor's degree. I knew I would have to go to summer school to reach my goal, and I didn't mind one bit. I was laser focused. I registered for eighteen credits which caused concern from my advisor. She was not happy about this. Rightfully, she didn't want me to burn out and flunk out. With some hesitation and a lot of persuasion, she approved my registration as long as I agreed to check in with her on a monthly basis.

One day, Ma noticed me buried behind a stack of books and asked, "Why are you taking so many classes your first semester? College is not a sprint. It's a marathon."

Shuffling piles of papers in front of me, I looked up and said, "You're supposed to finish high school in four years, right? Aren't you supposed to finish college in four years, too?"

"And it's ok if you don't. There's no need to kill your-self with stress. This is a new environment for you. Get acclimated."

Unfortunately, this over-achieving Virgo was not hearing any of it. Innately, I wanted to show my parents that I could do it despite changing schools. I wanted to make them proud.

THE DEDICATION

Chapter XII – Auditioning Sucks

I felt exhilarated and amazingly purposeful. I switched to part-time work at the factory and continued modeling and dancing. Auditions are unforgiving of time. If the casting is at 10:30 am, you are expected to be there at 10:15 am, ready to go. There's very little room for dancers holding down traditional nine-to-five jobs. You have to be available for callbacks, rehearsals, and fittings. Auditioning has a way of forcing humility down your throat. It's not for the thinned-skinned, and it's barely for the thick-skinned. Rejection can be painful, but sometimes it's necessary for growth. I'm reminded of the parting words a choreographer shared with me, "Never take rejection personally. The performance could be based on a specific look or a particular skill and talent. Simply do your best.

That's it. Allow whatever is meant to happen, happen." Those words forever stuck with me.

I heard about an audition for the Chicago Luvabulls and decided to give it a try. The NBA dance team for our beloved Chicago Bulls was an intense audition, one that took all day. I arrived at 8:00 am. I had to smile and be perky for eight straight hours or run the risk of being cut. It was ridiculous and nonsensical, yet, I wanted to be a part of the squad. I think I just wanted to dance at any cost, and I continued auditioning at warp speed. This audition was a familiar cattle call. The line wrapped around the block at 7:30 am. Luckily it was a summer day, so it was quite bearable waiting outside. I took my place in line behind a set of identical twins. Their skin was mocha complexion, and they had wide brown eyes. They looked more like models than dancers. I asked, "Has anyone come out and said anything?"

One of the sisters turned around and nodded, "Uh-Uh. We got here twenty minutes ago, and this line was already down the block. Can you believe it?"

"Wow!"

"Is this your first time trying out?"

"Yea. Is this your first?"

In sync, both girls responded, "No, this is our third."

I was stunned by this admission, and I guess my facial expression said it all.

One of the twins felt the need to justify and said, "We keep trying because we want to dance for the Bulls so bad. We heard that they just drafted this really great player. So, we shall see."

I gave a fake smile of encouragement and nodded. I turned around and noticed how quickly the line snaked behind me. There had to be at least 100 young ladies, if not more, all eager to dance. Stadium workers passed out numbered registration forms. Eighty-five was my audition number.

Upon entering, we lined up numerically to walk past the judges, and within fifteen minutes, the first cuts took place. Instantly, thirty-five girls were sent packing. Talk about a cattle call. They are ruthless. The first set of cuts was clearly based on physical appearance, how each dancer looked. I could not believe it! I noticed the twins quickly high fiving each other because they survived the first round. And just like that, we were down to eighty.

The captain introduced herself. She was wearing a full face of makeup and big hair at 8:00 am. I'm thinking, *"My God, why so much makeup. I could literally scrape two inches off. It's so thick."* I felt like I was back in a pageant. Turn it on. Turn it down. Turn it up. Smile, show teeth, smile some more. Show personality and

Never. Stop. Smiling.

Round two. The current squad performed and was really good. I always thought they got such a bad rep for not knowing how to dance, when actually, their technique was pretty good. It was a high-energy piece with lots of high kicks. The captain explained that everyone must audition, even the girls from last year's team. We learned a combination of splits, jumps, and leaps. It was, by no means, easy. It required stamina just to keep up. Oh, yeah, and don't forget to smile.

I replayed the steps quickly in my head for memorization. I did this a few times. Cool, I think I have it. I thought, here we go again. I took the floor when my number was called. One of the twins had just performed in the earlier group, and the other one was in my group. From the looks of it, the first twin struggled horribly. It was painful to watch. We took the floor and waited for the music to cue. Not gonna lie, I bodied that choreo. I knew it, and it showed. I exited the floor in a full-out sweat, panting, trying to catch my breath.

Luckily, I survived round two. Sadly, the twins did not. It was a huge cut. Around forty women were released. Out of the corner of my eye, I saw the beautiful twins crying, consoling each other as they quickly grabbed their things and exited the room. It was disheartening to see. They clearly wanted this so bad. I placed my emotions to the side to prepare for round three. This was the freestyle session. We had to improvise a four-set of eight counts. All while, you guessed it...SMILING!

Round three, done! Safe. "Thank you, Jesus," I whispered. It ended with the final elimination in round three.

Forty of us were chosen to represent the team for the upcoming season. We were elated! We cheered, hugged, and some, of course, cried tears of joy.

The director took center stage and said, "Congratulations, ladies. I know this was grueling, but you made it. We started with 137 women today, but we wanted the best of the best. You should be proud of yourselves. This is such an honor, but let me be clear, this is a professional job, and hard work is expected. There are a few important team rules I need to make you aware of right off the bat. Rule #1, No fraternizing with the players."

I instantly questioned fraternizing? While it was against the rules, I'm almost certain that it still occurred.

She continued, "Rule #2, you will receive a weekly weigh-in. So, if you have any extra weight, I'd suggest you start losing it now. Each month you're allowed a menstrual weight fluctuation of five pounds. I call it the period bloat."

I've never had a weight issue in my life unless you compare me to these stick-thin white girls. I'm sure I'm looking quite mammoth at five feet ten and 135 lbs.

"And Rule #3, while there are forty of you, only twenty will perform at each game. You will have a performance tryout every week. Twenty will make it, and twenty won't. If you're chosen to perform, the stipend is forty dollars per game. If you don't make it one week, you'll have another opportunity the following week. You only get paid if you dance. Is this clear? Which brings me to Rule#4 you must work a full-time job or attend school full time. Because forty dollars is definitely NOT a livable wage."

I glanced around the room. Is anyone growing livid at the outrageous demands? I'm thinking, *"You've got to be kidding me."* With forty dollars, you won't have money for food, guaranteeing your ass will stay skinny. This was asinine. The players rack in millions. Yet we will have to starve ourselves, work a regular nine to five, practice late hours with the fifty-fifty chance of being chosen to dance. All for a funky forty dollars? And just when you thought it couldn't get any more disrespectful, I'm not allowed to date any of the players, should an opportunity arise? I wanted to shout, '*Fuck You, Lady!'*

The captain continued, "Are there any questions? Remember, this is a privileged opportunity." We sat motionless with our smile still plastered, just happy as a clam to be called a Luvabull. No one said a single word, but I was sure thinking of a few colorful words I wanted to use.

"This is such an honor to say, Congratulations on being chosen for the upcoming Chicago Bulls season." Applause and acclamation erupted for the director.

This didn't sit right with me, and I was bothered by what I heard. To be honest, it was downright humiliating. I kept thinking about the period pounds. How disrespectful was that? But in that egregious moment, I retreated. Deep down, this was bullshit, and I knew it.

After an exhausting day, I finally made it home. "Ma, I made it!" I mean, on one hand, it was nice to finally make a grueling audition. However, on the other hand, this gig SUCKED! Denice was in Ma's room. "I made the Luvabulls team."

"What's a Luvabulls?" Ma said,

"The cheerleaders for the Chicago Bulls. Don't you know that?"

"That's so great. You were there all this time?"

"Yeah, there were over 100 girls, 137 to be exact."

"How many girls did they pick?"

"Only forty."

"Do they pay y'all?"

"Yea, forty dollars per game."

Denice stopped what she was doing. "What? Forty dollars!"

I was embarrassed saying it out loud. Denice was a straightforward type of chick who did not mince her words.

"So, you're telling me, the players get all that money, and they can only pay y'all a stingy forty dollars? That is ridiculously ludicrous!"

I pretended like it didn't matter. As a supportive parent, Ma was not about to deflate my aspirational balloon.

She didn't respond to Denice's redundancy, even though she, too, knew it was dreadful.

"Well, what does the rehearsal schedule look like?"

"It's twice per week, 7:00 pm–10:00 pm."

"That's a huge time commitment. Don't forget about school."

"I know. I'll manage."

Denice interjected, "Please tell me that they at least pay y'all for rehearsals?" I ignored her contemptuous remarks because I really wanted to be a Luvabull, or so I thought.

The first rehearsal was extreme. We were weighed every Wednesday with an allowable five-pound menstrual gain. Talk about the toxic disrespect. We danced from 7:00 pm until 10:00 pm. Exhaustion was an understatement. I crashed when I got home. Dad would peek into my room and see me sprawled on my bed. He was a "Proud Dad," and I was dead tired.

The following week, after practice, I heard an audition announcement on the radio, *"Dream Girls audition September 22nd, looking for singers, dancers, and actors. Please report to Kennedy-King, Katherine Dunham Theater, to showcase your talent. Call 312-602-5000 for more information."* I had butterflies just writing the information down. I took this energy as an omen, reflecting if I should go or not.

I was in awe of how quickly my new life was falling into place. I transferred schools, declared a major, and was dancing for our beloved Chicago Bulls. It's something about trusting the universe because the foundation of my faith was instilled by my spiritual upbringing. We were expected to attend church services every week. Daddy never went, but Ma did. A repetitive spiritual theme was to trust yourself to take two steps and have faith that God would take four steps on your behalf. It's not about knowing; it is about believing. I still subscribe to this belief.

I managed my school classes and continued my dance training. Deciding to take eighteen credit hours was academic insanity, but by the grace of God, I pulled it off. I was firmly committed to a four-year graduation timeline. Having completed two years at Western, I only had two years left to get all my requirements completed.

To stay on track, I was forced to meticulously map out every single course, seminar, workshop, project, and internship required to earn my bachelor's degree. I had to be copious and strategic. My personal notebook housed my methodical plan. I would obsess over it to stay on target. Once again, my advisor did not want to sign off on my schedule, but I'm pretty convincing when I have to be.

The weekly Luvabull rehearsals intensified as we prepped a month before our first season opener. I couldn't shake the Dreamgirls audition and kept thinking about it, day in and day out. There's no way I could find time to insert anything else in my schedule. Then again, this didn't stop me from trying.

I was in grind mode. I gathered my headshot and decided to go to the Dreamgirls audition anyway. Upon arriving at the theater, a voice echoed, "If you're here for the role of dancer, please take ten minutes to warm up. The director is Phil Landing, and Bobby Luckett is the choreographer. Both will be out shortly to get started."

I closed my eyes to channel the energy of the original Broadway cast production. Jennifer Holiday, Loretta Devine, Sheryl Lee Ralph, Vondie Curtis-Hall, and Donald Cohen, Obba Babatunde, encapsulated my spirit and affirmed I was right where I was supposed to be in that moment. I took a deep breath to inhale for those who came before and exhale for those who will come after me. It was a moment of profound gratitude.

"Excuse me, Miss, Miss?"

Startled, I opened my eyes.

The young lady said, "I didn't want to interrupt your meditation, but I need your headshot." I yanked one out of my portfolio and handed it to her. "By the way, I'm Debra, the stage director, costume assistant, and casting assistant. You name it, and I do it."

"I'm Patrice."

Debra was full of energy and friendly. "Are you auditioning for the role of dancer?"

"Yes, I am."

"I thought so. You definitely look like a dancer."

There were about twenty dancers. I had no idea how many they were selecting for the production. After briefly stretching my body, we were divided into two groups to learn the choreography. It wasn't too difficult or technical. However, the movement had to be exaggerated and bold for stage musicals and plays. Otherwise, the stage would swallow your performance. I practiced the movement first mentally and then full out. Each group performed twice for the director. The choreographer jotted down the director's rambling remarks. I felt good about my performance.

The director spoke, "Thank you for auditioning for Dreamgirls. In case you didn't know, this production will provide equity points."

I had no idea what equity points were, but it must have been worth mentioning by the dancers and actors' responses. They lit up with this information.

He continued, "If you are chosen, we will work hard to prepare for opening night, which is only six weeks away. Previews will begin on December 14. If we liked what we saw tonight, you will get a callback later this week. There's not much time, and we will need to move fast. We will perform five shows per week. Wednesday through Sunday." You could hear the anticipation from the mixed crowd of men and women. "Are there any questions?"

A lady with the killer body of Jessica Rabbit raised her hand. I glanced her over. I remembered her because she auditioned in my group. She looked familiar. Petite, maybe, five foot three. She was stunning with a voluptuous shape.

"Yes, Zelda." The director knew her by name. She must be a professional.

"What will the rehearsal schedule consist of?" She was confident and self-assured. She must have worked with the director before.

The director said, "Tuesday, Wednesday, and Thursday, 6:00 pm–9:00 pm, with add-on days the closer we get to opening night."

Zelda jotted notes in a binder. I'm watching her because maybe she reminds me of someone else. But who? There were 100 girls at the Luvabull audition; maybe that's why she looks recognizable. I couldn't pinpoint it, so I let it go.

Bobby stuck to Phil's side as they continued to whisper notes about each dancer. When he finished, he added, "Once again, thank you for coming."

It was late, so I hurried to gather my things. All I could think about was if I'm chosen, this will definitely create a scheduling conflict with my Luvabulls practice. As I headed to the parking lot, I heard a voice.

"Hey?" I looked back; it was Ms. Bunny herself. "Wait up a minute. You know you were really good. I'm sure you made it," she said reassuringly. "I'm Zelda."

"Really? You think so?" I asked.

"Oh yeah, they were mesmerized by your performance. Plus, look at you? You're tall and beautiful."

"I'm Patrice, and thank you for the kind words, but sometimes you just never know. You were too." I appreciated the vote of confidence, but my confidence hadn't peaked at that level yet.

"Have you worked with the director before? They definitely knew you. That should make you feel great, plus look at you; you are stunning." It was humanizing to realize I wasn't the only one who experienced insecurities.

"Sorry for staring, but I know you from somewhere. Did you audition for the Luvabull?"

"Heck no! The pay is crap, and they work you like a workhorse. No thank you, it definitely wasn't me."

"Maybe, it'll come to me."

"They say we all have a twin somewhere in the world."

"True. True. How do you know the director?"

"I worked with both of them before. Phil is a genius. He's been nominated for Jeff Awards throughout the theater community, and he always hires Bobby to choreograph his shows. I've performed with both of them in 'Don't Bother Me, I Can't Cope, and in Chicago.'"

I was impressed with her level of theatrical experience. "If I were you, I wouldn't worry about it too much. I think you were pretty fabulous, and boy, did you serve them body? No one here tonight gave them sex appeal like you."

"Use it or lose it, is what I always say," Zelda smirked.

"I guess."

We continued laughing as we walked to our cars. She was naturally friendly, not the forced, fake kind. It was refreshing, especially in such a competitive field.

"If we both make it, I'll see you at rehearsal."

"You mean, *when* we both make it."

Zelda agreed. "I like the sound of that." As she turned to get in her car, I saw what appeared to be a tattoo down the side of her neck. My memory instantly flashed back to the teenager who quickly exited the studio at Sammy Dyer as I arrived on my first day of class. The V-shaped mark on the side of her neck revealed the very talented dancer that inspired me at the Sammy Dyer. Zelda was that girl in the studio many years ago.

Ma was always the first to ask me about any of my auditions. Honestly, the only one to ask. Probably the only one who knew I actually had an audition.

"How did it go? You were there pretty late."

"It went really well, but you just never know. The director said we should hear something later this week. It's a grueling schedule, but it sounds exciting. They seemed to like me, so we shall see."

Ma reassured me, "Of course they liked you, and as your dad would say, *"How could they not?"*

In unison, we said, "Cuz you're a Kuykendal!" Daddy was Kuykendal proud and he made sure to remind us of our superpower.

Even though Ma was my number one fan, she secretly worried if I was doing too much, too fast, too soon. She asked, "Would you be able to do that and the Chicago Bulls?"

I sighed and rubbed my forehead. "I don't think so. I may have to choose." She supported me no matter what. My happiness was all that mattered. I remember asking her what if I wanted to do Playboy magazine, and not surprisingly, she said, "Go for it! Why not?" I wasn't actually thinking about doing Playboy. I just wanted to see what her response would be. Mom was indeed something else. Now, dad, that would have been an altogether different convo.

The following day, I had almost forgotten my scheduled conference with my advisor. I rushed through her door, making it barely in time. And like always, she expressed her discourse in my ability to sustain my full-time class schedule. She saw the weight in my eyes as I slumped down in her office chair, half-listening to her lecture on academia burnout. Today just wasn't the day. I was dog-tired, so I politely excused myself to run and catch the 6:25 pm bus home.

"I'm sorry she's not here. Would you like to leave a message?" The voice on the receiver continued to talk. Denice jotted a message on a notepad and tossed it aside. As soon as I walked through the door, Denice yelled, "You got a message on the counter."

"Thanks, my slave. When did they call?"

She ignored me. "Good help is so hard to find," I snapped and dialed the number. "Hello, this is Patrice Kuykendal returning a phone call."

The lady began, "Ms. Patrice, you recently auditioned for Dreamgirls at The Katherine Dunham Theater?"

"Yes."

"I'm calling from the Katherine Dunham Theater. You have been chosen as a dancer for Dreamgirls. Congratulations!"

"Thank you!"

"Are you accepting the role?"

I couldn't contain my joy. "Absolutely!"

"Wonderful! The director and choreographer are looking forward to working with you. They thought you were great. Rehearsals will begin next week. You will get another call with all the details."

"Ok, thank you. I'm so excited." I hung up the phone with Ma staring directly at me.

"What?" I asked.

"How on earth are you going to fulfill all these commitments?"

"I don't know yet. The Luvabulls and Dreamgirls rehearse at the same time." Ma continued to stare at me, clearly not satisfied with my response. "Don't take on too much and get overwhelmed."

"I know, I know, I won't."

This wasn't a tough decision. I was more excited about making the Luvabull audition than actually being on the squad. Out of 137 girls, I was one of the chosen few. I made the cut. The weekly weigh-ins were downgrading and humiliating. They were quietly contributing to a culture of body insecurity and eating disorders. I was happy to relieve myself of that responsibility.

As an upcoming dancer, you quickly learn that most people will take your gift for granted. Repeatedly I was told, "There's no pay, but it's a great way to acquire exposure as a new dancer." Yes, I was new on the audition circa, but my talent, aptitude, and work ethic were enough. This paradigm shift elevated my esteem and changed the trajectory of my dance journey. I happily re-signed from the Luvabulls and never looked back. I joined the cast of Dreamgirls, ready to leave my mark in musical theater.

Rehearsals were long and demanding. As a novice in the theater world, I took my role seriously. I took everything in. I studied the direction, staging, the sound, musical elements, and blocking. I was so enthralled with every aspect of the production that before you knew it, I was learning the roles of the understudies. I was treated as a professional in this environment, and Zelda and I became close friends. We were always together, preparing, reviewing, and rehearsing. I learned a lot from her. She was genuine with way more theatrical experience than me.

The cast was a group of hilarious, talented individuals who, without question, should have all earned an EGOT: Emmy, Grammy, Oscar, and Tony. They were divas waiting in the wings for their big break. Such an immensely talented group of individuals. I was honored they allowed this newcomer into their tightly knit artistic circle.

"Patrice, is that you?" As soon as I turned, someone grabbed my hand and hoisted me into the air.

"Oh my, God!" It was Keith.

"What are you doing here?"

"I was brought in as one of the dancers. Are you in this production too?"

"Yeah. The second week of rehearsal," I said, smiling. Zelda looked from the sideline. I introduced them, "Keith, this is Zelda."

Abruptly, Zelda facetiously interrupted, "Oh, I know Keith."

"Yes, Ms. Zelda, how have you been?"

"How have I been? More like, how have YOU been, Mr. Keith?"

These two clearly had a contentious history. "I'm good. Still taking classes from Tommy. Matter of fact, that's where I met Patrice. She was studying with Tommy, too, on 55th Street." Zelda sucked her teeth and walked away.

With Keith still holding my hand, I coyly managed to untangle my fingers from his grip. He turned all his attention towards me.

"You hardly come to class anymore. I asked Tommy when the last time you were there."

"I know. I need to get back asap. I've been really busy. I transferred from Western, and it's been kicking my butt. I've been dancing on the westside too. You heard of Bob Richardson?" I sounded like a rambling schoolgirl.

"Of course, I have. Former Ailey dancer. Teaches out of the dome, right?" "Yea, that's him."

"I used to dance with him back in the day, but we fell out. He owed me money from a show. So be careful."

"I hope to get back to classes right after Dreamgirls closes."

"You do have a lot going on. I was hoping I didn't run you away."

I pursed my lips, thinking, *"Here we go."* Instantly, my body became flushed, and I simply laughed off his ridiculous claims.

Bobby announced, "Break is officially over, and before we start again, I'd like to introduce our newest member to the Dreamgirl family. For those that already know, Keith is a dance extraordinaire. He'll be joining the cast as CC, and he'll also take over the role of dance captain in my absence." We all applauded this news, except for Zelda. She stood off solemnly while the rest of us congratulated Keith.

Zelda and I always left rehearsal together. It was dark, so we would intentionally park next to each other to avoid having to walk solo. Today, she must have left immediately because I caught a glimpse of her car pulling out of the parking lot. I shrugged it off and got into my car. As I reached to close the door, a hand grabbed the window and blocked my view. It was dark and difficult to see. The shadowy figure loomed in closer. My heart skipped several beats, and I couldn't process what was happening.

Suddenly, a voice emerged. "No goodbyes? You were gonna just leave without saying goodbye?"

I screamed, "Keith! Shit! You scared me!"

"I'm sorry. I looked for you and thought you were gone."

It took a few beats to regain my composure. My breathing consumed me. I tried to temper my physical and emotional reaction because my adrenaline had shot through the roof.

Keith noticed me physically shaking. "I really am sorry. Do you mind if I get in?" He lifted both hands in the air. "No more antics, I promise." I popped the locks to open the doors.

"Patrice, it's really great seeing you. I kept hoping you would use that number I gave you."

"Keith, I just haven't found time. Trying to get my footing in this thing called life. And with school, I'm carrying a full load."   Keith was handsomely attractive, but my gaydar was on high alert with most male dancers. Many were either gay or bisexual, and I wasn't categorically attracted to either subgroup. "Keith, what was up with you and Zelda? It's obvious there's history between you two."

He took a long pause. "It's a long story, but the short version is...we dated. It didn't work out. Now she hates me. The end. If she tells you anything different, don't believe any of it. She's bitter Betsy."

181

"As they say, there are three sides to every story." Besides, I considered Zelda a friend. "It's late, and I need to be going."

He leaned in closer, whispering, "You can't hide from me now. I thought about you so much, Patrice."

I quickly turned my head to prevent his full-on mouth attempt at a kiss. He caught my cheek. I popped the lock to make sure it was unlocked. "I need to go, Keith."

He finally got out of the car. "I won't hold you hostage, any longer."

"Whatever," I rolled my eyes and pulled out of the lot.

For the next couple of weeks at rehearsal, I avoided Keith's flirtatious banter. His behavior made me uncomfortable at times because it was obvious, he was vying for my attention. Thankfully, he eventually got the message and moved on to another dancer. This time to a male dancer.

The director gave me the additional role of swing, so I needed to focus. There was so much more to learn. I was now responsible for multiple parts, including choreography and blocking. I had to be ready in the event someone was not able to go on—kind of like an understudy but more of an ensemble member. This was my very first professional theater gig, and I wanted to shine. No, I had to shine. The stage was comfortable, and it felt like home. I fell in love with the entire production: the costumes, music, songs, lighting, staging, script, and the cast.

The closer we got to opening night, the more concentrated our rehearsals became. Tech rehearsals were excruciatingly long, sometimes not finishing until midnight. I began to bring my schoolwork to the theater to complete during downtime or when I wasn't needed on stage. I had papers and assignments still due, which caused me to treat my course syllabus like the holy grail. But I stayed on top of my class assignments, making sure I met all deadlines.

Anxiety was running high on preview night. The auditorium was filled with every industry critic and journalist, including the entire Kuykendal Klan. During previews, we received rave reviews from Hannity Weiss and notable mentions from other artistic columnists. In the theater community, the play was a huge success and was nominated for many Jeff Awards. There was talk about extending our run and a possible tour. Unfortunately, it never panned out. I'm forever indebted to the magical memories of Dreamgirls. The cast and crew taught me so much. It is understandable how theater could become such an addictive form of art.

Armed with a new entry on my headshot and resume, naturally, I wanted to audition more. A new person emerged as a result of my Dreamgirls experience. I became more confident. Commanding attention when I walked into an audition. Every opportunity was grounded in growth. The more I auditioned, the better I became. I enhanced my appearance with wigs, hairpieces, and professional makeup. I no longer hid in the back of the room.

I made sure to take center stage so the directors, agents, and choreographers would see me and recognize my talent.

I patiently watched and learned. The more I watched, the more I learned, and ultimately, I began getting callbacks, securing more dance gigs. I continued dancing with Bob, finally perfecting his duet. Greg and I performed the *First Time Ever I Saw Your Face by* Roberta Flack during a bridal convention. The attendees could not get enough of the performance. It was beautiful choreography to perform. It was emotional and sensual. We danced like euphoric lovers experiencing the purest form of unadulterated joy. It told the affair of a hypnotic entanglement of the hearts. One that would ultimately *last until the end of time.*

THE DEDICATION

Chapter XIII — Changing Times

The warmth of my neighborhood was slowly dissipating. The quiet streetlights of fading laughter were replaced with an occasional distant gunshot. New neighbors moved in, and old ones contemplated moving out, us included. I would often hear late-night discussions of the suburban shift. I honestly never thought it would happen, though. Our block was our refuge. It was where we felt safe. But as they say, change is indeed inevitable. It was in the dark era of a new dawning. And as much as I didn't want to admit it, the neighborhood was experiencing an eerie shift.

Bub was now a full-fledged teenager in high school, and as a young black male, my parents worried about his development. Being old enough to remember stories about the police corruption, where innocent black and brown men were brutally tortured into false confessions. Not to mention the ascension to power by some of Chicago's toughest rival gang leaders. Rightfully, my parents worried every time he left the house. Because of this, they decided to enroll Bub in Leo Catholic High School, in hopes the priests and nuns could influence a mature moral development. The catholic schools were strict. The boys had to wear ties as part of their school uniform. Demerits and detention were given if students were not properly dressed. On any given afternoon, when the bell rang, you would see students frantically snatching their neckties off as soon as their feet hit the sidewalk pavement.

A close friend of our family also sent their son Johnathan to private school for the same reasons, and Bub and Johnathan became best friends. The dynamics were different in raising boys than girls, and I understood why. The streets were changing, and parents wanted to protect their children at all costs. Johnathan enrolled first, and Bub quickly followed suit. It also happened to be the alma mater of Darice's star athlete boyfriend, Randy. Leo fostered a rigorous program, both academically and athletically. It was an all-male, mass attending, priest greeting, communion having, tie and khakis wearing highly regarded institution on the south side of Chicago.

A few years ago, Bub befriended a new kid to the block, who they called Lil TP. It was short for Thomas Payne, named after his dad. He was three years younger, sweet, respectful, and he idolized Bub. I think he was an only child, so he took to Bub instantly. You could easily find Lil TP at our house at least three times per week, eating, laughing, and playing video games. His family was originally from the west side and seemed to have settled nicely in the community. Startled by the sound of the doorbell, I was in a daze, listening to music while cleaning the kitchen. I glanced at the back door to see one of Bub's confidantes standing behind the screen door. It was November and the weather wasn't cold-cold, but it was chilly enough for a heavy jacket. I opened the door.

"Bub here?" Lil TP asked. I unlocked the screen and opened the door.

"You already know where he is."

Lil TP knew the layout of our house. He walked through the kitchen, past the dining room, and straight down the stairs to the basement. Minutes later, you could hear the laughter and noise filtering through the vents. This was their norm. Lil TP stayed many hours at our house. However, Bub seldomly trekked to his building, which was only a few houses away.

On this particular visit, Lil TP exited the basement door. I remember the sun was still shining. However, the exact time escapes me. An hour or so could have passed before I heard what sounded like firecrackers through an open window. The M-80 ones. They sounded like gunshots or mini-explosions. Afterward came a distinct scream. I literally froze because of the piercing sound. I ran to the front window and saw people running in the same direction. In the midst of the chatter and confusion, I kept hearing the crowd saying, "Tee, Tee, Tee." Gunfire has its own unique salient sound.

Ma asked, "Did you hear that?"

I nodded in agreement. "Everyone is running. I think someone has been shot. At first, it sounded like fireworks." Ma just shook her head in disbelief. No more than five minutes elapsed when I heard our neighbors scream, "No!" I was greeted by sirens as I stepped outside. My neighbors confirmed it was Lil TP. The deafening police sirens drowned out the wailing and screams. A neighbor pointed. TP's body had collapsed between the alley and garage with maybe three or four fatal gunshots. His body lay on the ground. I tried to look away but recognized the tip of his shoe. I headed home with tears streaming. "Ma, it was Lil TP."

I didn't have my room dawg to lean on for support. Darice was away attending an HBCU in Ohio. Her star athlete boyfriend repped the Buckeyes, and she wanted to be as close to him as possible. Ma and daddy agreed to let her go to Central State University in Wilberforce, Ohio. As long as she was in school, all was well with them. I missed our nonstop laughter and inside jokes.

School was going fine. I stayed on top of my assignments, determined not to fall behind. A commuter school is so different from a campus environment. In the city, there wasn't time to build relationships even though networking is everything. It was truly a rat race. I took the bus and L train downtown every morning. I fought the crowds on public transportation to get to class on time. My professors were working professionals in the industry who could provide the ins and outs of breaking into the business. My peers often filled the halls as chain smokers to pass the fifteen minutes between classes. Maybe the idea of attending school in the city stressed them out. I only hoped the secondhand smoke wouldn't kill me in this poorly ventilated building. In comparison, I don't recall seeing students on the yard light up profusely.

The manicured and immaculate landscape on Western's campus was quite soothing and serene in retrospect. Unlike the seedy landfill you had to pass on the train ride or the pick-pocketers you came to know because of their familiar rush hour routine.

Time flew by in the city. There was never enough of it. Still, being home provided an abundance of opportunities and endless possibilities. I was determined to take advantage of them all. I was busy and I liked it this way. My purpose was no longer futile. I woke up every day determined to live a life well-lived. I eventually quit working at Soft Sheen because I started to feel stretched. My parents were ok with this, but I knew eventually, I'd find another part-time job as soon as the semester ended.

THE DESTINY

Chapter XIV – Interviewing

I finished my first year with a modest 3.2 GPA, which was pretty remarkable considering everything I had going on. I went to summer school at a community college to continue my goal of obtaining my degree in four years. I hated summer school. It was blasphemous to have to attend on such beautiful warm summer nights in Chicago.

In my last year at Columbia, I took the following classes: Writing for television, production, and public relations. Securing an internship was a requirement for all would-be graduates. This would help get your foot in the door by establishing contacts and networking in the industry. Columbia had an amazing job board and did a terrific job at selling expensive dreams. However, the onus was on each student to make them come true. This demanded discovery, development, decision-making, determination, and drive.

I would check the board every day, and finally an intriguing posting caught my eye. In bold typeface, it stated, "Chicago Cable Commission seeks energetic intern to assist with various upcoming productions and projects. Serious inquiries only." It didn't sound sexy, but I was running out of options. I secured an interview at the Streeterville office. I mean, who wouldn't want free labor, right? An internship forces you to work without pay in hopes of securing future employment. I rushed out of class to hop on the #124 bus. I definitely didn't want to be late and make a piss-poor first impression.

Rush hour was starting, and the bus was already packed. I watched each stop closely, silently praying for all green traffic lights. I stepped off the bus, fluffed my hair, and tried to smooth out my noticeable wrinkles. I looked down at the address. I was only two blocks away. "Perfect!" I breathed a sigh of relief as I walked briskly to make it on time. The building was somewhat antiquated, but the neighborhood was quickly becoming one of the most expensive zip codes in the city. I waited for the elevator, and as I stepped off, pictures of past mayors greeted me. I only recognized Daley and our beloved Harold Washington on the wall. Washington was the first black mayor of Chicago, and we loved him deeply. I introduced myself to the receptionist.

"Hello, I'm Patrice Kuykendal. I have an interview for the internship with Commissioner Ware." She had a pleasant smile and soft eyes.

"Yes, I spoke to you on the phone. Commissioner Ware is expecting you. Please have a seat."

"Thank you."

I took a quick look out the window. The view was breathtaking. You could actually see Navy Pier and Lake Michigan. I stared at the waves crashing against the pier. It was captivating.

The receptionist interrupted my daze. "He's ready to see you now." She led me to his office and closed the door behind me.

A tall, strikingly handsome African American male walked toward me with his hand extended. "I'm Commissioner Ware."

"Patrice Kuykendal. Nice to meet you."

Even though he was old enough to be my father, he was definitely easy on the eyes. I shook his hand and thanked him for meeting with me.

"Please have a seat. You're here for the internship, correct?"

"Yes, I am."

"Which school?"

"Columbia. Not to be confused with the leaf Sir, Columbia Chicago." He grinned a charming smile. I thought, *"Great, he got my joke."* I turned on the charm.

"Patrice, please tell me something about yourself… something that I might find particularly interesting and surprising at the same time."

I was prepared and well-rehearsed. Must be the pageantry in me. I took a deep breath and exhaled. "First, thank you for taking time out of your busy schedule to meet with me, Commissioner Ware. I'm in my last year, studying television production with a minor in communication."

He interrupted, "Fascinating."

"I'm also a dancer. I call it my professional hobby." The commissioner looked genuinely curious.

"Really?" he noted. "What type of dance do you do?"

Whenever I get this question from a guy, I think their mind instantly detours to stripping. He probably was no different.

"Well, sir, I've studied ballet, modern, tap, and many different techniques and genres." Immediately, I got creepy old-man vibes and regretted bringing it up.

"Are you any good?"

"Well, yes, I like to think so." I tried to reign the conversation in.

"So, what would you like to do with it?" The commissioner's grin became wider.

"There are so many facets in television. I'm interested in learning as much as I can, particularly in the area of producing."

"No, no...I mean with dance. It seems like you've been studying dance for a long time."

"Matter of fact Mr. Commissioner, I just finished Dreamgirls at the Katherine Dunham Theater."

Leaning comfortably in his leather executive chair, he swayed slowly from side to side, smiling.

I interrupted his glare. "Excuse me, Commissioner Ware, can you tell me what you're looking for in an intern and what are some of the responsibilities?"

Unamused, he swiveled his chair in his corner office to face the sun gleaming off the lake. "Sometimes it's crazy long hours in unbearable conditions. We need dependable punctual individuals." He pivoted his chair to face me again. "You'll gain experience behind the camera, logging cables, and we may even let you get some directing in. I have an excellent crew. Matter of fact, if you join us, you'll be the only female. Would you be comfortable in that kind of environment?" He paused.

I answered very directly. I needed him to know, I could hold my own. "Absolutely, Sir."

"Great." He shook my hand and held it five seconds too long.

I was offered the internship position. My advisor was pleased and reminded me of the many contacts and networking opportunities with the city of Chicago's Cable Division.

I reported to a man named David. David was middle-aged, maybe five foot six, with red hair and wore squared glasses. He managed the crew members like a coach, always ending his talks with a motivating sermon. He was firm and encouraging. I didn't really mind being the only girl in the crew. As long as I was respected and treated fairly, I was good.

Day one, I was handed my credentials stamped, *All Access*. David said strongly, "Do. Not. Lose. This. Ever. This badge will allow you entry anywhere in the city, understood?"

"Yes,"

The four of us loaded into a van specifically marked "Property of the City of Chicago." It was a nondescript Ford with plenty of storage space. To show chivalry wasn't dead, the guys let me take the front seat.

"You have your license?" David asked.

"Yes, sir, I do." I wanted to be professional, so I tried to gauge the culture of my new colleagues.

The guys rolled with laughter as one of them said, "Patrice, relax you got the job already, and besides, David's not a sir." Raul was the most boisterous one. He was muscular in build looked to be in his late twenties. The laughter didn't let up. The guys clowned each other pretty much all day. For the next four months, I had to put up with their teasing. It was all in jest, and after getting used to their childish antics, they were actually a fun group to work with.

For my first official job, we packed the van with tape cassettes, cameras, stands, various mics, audio, and video cables. It reminded me of the equipment used at school. Definitely not state-of-the-art. David spoke the entire fifteen-minute ride. "Patrice, wear your credentials around your neck. We are required to film all of the mayor's boring press conferences, but don't worry, sometimes, we get to work a few fun events too. Regardless, we always give 110 percent."

I took it all in. As the new kid on the set, I was relatively quiet. I did way more listening than talking. As soon as we pulled in front of city hall, the guys jumped out, grabbing all the equipment. They moved so fast my head was spinning. I jumped out of the way to prevent being knocked down or ran over by the crew. I thought, "Boy, I have to get used to this speed."

David called out. "Patrice, your credentials, don't forget them."

I snatched them from my work bag and threw them around my neck. We took our spot for the press conference.

Lloyd, another member of our team, forgot the cable and shouted. "Patrice, quick, I need you to run to the van and grab the cable from the trunk."

"Ok, sure!" I was a nervous wreck. I darted to the van, grabbed the cable, and ran back inside. Lloyd gave me a thumb's up and connected the wires to the cable. Raul made sure all the cables stayed connected throughout the presser.

The wise-cracking jokes stopped when the mayor entered the room. It was all business, as reporters competed to get their questions answered. Our job was to tape, not report. Our footage would air on the city's cable access channel. Still, I was alongside network affiliates of all the major stations. There was ABC, CBS, NBC, FOX, plus a host of smaller independent media outlets. Listening to the mayor speak on the upcoming festival season wasn't actually newsworthy, but just to be in the same space with these major players made it all worth it.

I went home that day with my chest slightly puffed out. Day one of my internship, checked! The crew became like family, and everyone treated me like their baby sister, very protective. When one of us forgot to pack something, they trusted me to drive the company car back and forth to the office. I was even given time behind the camera lens.

My internship extended past the semester, and my advisor was elated they wanted to hire me as a freelancer. Although the summer hours were treacherous, the pay and experience were worth it. From sunup to sundown, we were assigned to tape every festival in the city. Who knew there was such a thing called the Pierogi Fest? Imagine looking through the lens of a camera for eight straight hours, sometimes longer in the hot melting sun during Gospel Fest, Blues Fest, Jazz Fest, Taste of Chicago, and the other gazillion local neighborhood festivals. I was grateful for the opportunity, and the guys taught me a lot. I agreed to the work and committed myself 110%.

My team depended on me and was impressed with my work ethic. David even mentioned it to the commissioner during one of our staff meetings. "Patrice has been phenomenal! She's a real class act and has no problem pulling her weight."

As the only girl in the room, I felt slightly embarrassed. Everyone applauded. I can handle the attention of gawkers when I'm on stage, but when I'm not performing, I consider myself to be very reserved, avoiding unwanted attention. On the one hand, I could literally dance and perform in front of tens of thousands of people, but on the other hand, I consider myself somewhat distant and aloof. When people find out I'm a dancer, they expect me to be an extrovert, "on" all the time. I consider myself an introvert, secretly living life as an extrovert. As a matter of fact, I find attention-seeking people to be needy and insecure. I managed a forced smile to David's compliments.

"Great job, Patrice," the commissioner said. "I'm sure you've heard the city is hosting All-Star this year." I hadn't. I looked over at Raul taking an air swing with an imaginary baseball bat. "...and the mayor provided us with on the field credentials."

Raul joked, "Guess all that schmoozing paid off." The guys were ecstatic.

In no way am I a baseball fan, so it was just another gig. For me, the game is entirely too long, too slow, and too boring. Who cares if it is the All-Star? Apparently, these guys did. Slapping high fives all over the place. The All-Star was a week away, yet these grown men had turned into giddy little schoolboys in anticipation.

We reported to the office to receive our daily work assignment. Lucky me (and I mean that with every bit of contrite sarcasm), I was working the All-Star opening ceremony. David was all smiles. He even spruced up his casual attire. The guys teased him, of course. "Patrice, you'll be working the All-Star with me." He cautiously handed me my lanyard embossed with "All-Access MLB All-Star 1990."

By now, I was used to the drill. I interrupted, "I know, I know, don't lose it." Today, I would have been perfectly content working the Randolph Street or Back of the Yards festival. I mean, it was an exciting event for the city. It's just that baseball wasn't my thing.

We arrived at the Wrigley Field's press entrance, flashed our lanyard, and headed to the media tent. The spread was outstanding. The guys dived straight in, grabbing sandwiches, desserts, and drinks. I didn't eat a thing. Some of the star athletes were engaged in interviews, jesting with the reporters. Others were occupied with hamming it up for the photogs. You could sense the excitement and elation. I was one of the very few females in this male-dominated arena.

Raul whispered, "This is so surreal. You know who that is, right?" A squinted eyebrow told him I didn't. He pointed to an older-looking man smiling for the camera. "It's Mr. Baseball himself, Ernie Banks, live and in the flesh." After a few pictures, Mr. Banks was escorted to the mound for the first ceremonial pitch. Raul's mouth dropped open. He had died and gone to baseball heaven. He was on top of the world.

I had to admit being in the center of the hoopla gave me more appreciation of the sport. I wasn't instantly converted into a fan, but it was humbling to see some of the larger local networks set their cameras right next to mine. Daddy was indeed a fan of baseball and couldn't believe I was actually on the mound with the players. In his eyes, I had made it to the major leagues without a doubt.

I graduated magna cum laude with a 3.5 GPA. Freelancing was cute, but I longed for something more concrete and stable. I continue to check the school's job board for leads. Every day, I would peruse the television division, anxiously, scanning the announcements in search of a position in television. Occasionally, I'd peak at the dance notices for sheer inspiration. After a couple of months of nonstop interviewing, nothing materialized. I longed for my big break into the industry. I had to get my foot in the door. It was taking a little longer than I anticipated. I wanted steady pay with benefits. So, I knew I needed to carefully strategize my next career move. I was young. I was hungry. I was determined. I was ready to work.

My oldest sister was steadily working at a bank, and they were hiring part-timers. I decided it was time to get a job. I reasoned by telling myself this would be temporary until Hollywood starts ringing my phone. Although it was a part-time position, it provided benefits. I applied and was hired. By working at the bank, I understood how easy it is to walk away from your goals, aspirations, and dreams. Lucky for me, I only carried a few bills. My student loans weren't due yet, and I was still living at home.

Ma reminded me that patience is a virtue, and all things happen in divine order. She carefully warned me not to become frustrated because I thought life would happen so quickly and easily. I held on to my dreams tightly and recommitted myself to keep trying.

As an alumnus, I was able to continue to use the student career resources. However, the onus was on me. If I was going to make it happen, I had to take ownership and responsibility for my successes and for my failures. I was going to reap the invested benefits of seeds sown. How could I earnestly expect 100 percent if I only invested 50 percent in myself? On most days, I would head straight to career services at the end of my work shift from the bank. I could be found on the third floor looking, exploring, and researching companies in the entertainment sector. I allowed the wise words from my mother to replay over in my head. Of course, I never imagined my dreams of working in television would lead me to work as a bank teller, but it paid the bills.

Being a bank teller wasn't exactly a horrible job, except you were required to stand on your feet all day. Now that was exhausting! Plus, the daily toll of riding overcrowded public transportation had you fighting through rush-hour crowds because you could never find an empty seat.

Dad yells for me as soon as I walk through the door. "Patrice, come here." My father was clever with his phrasing. He would never ask you to do things. He had this way of telling you what you were about to do, a communication style I came to emulate and appreciate later in life. He said, "Go get my lotteries." I shrieked. "Daddy, I'm *JUST* getting home. Denice and Darice, they've been here all day. Ughhhhhhh!" He didn't care and handed me his numbers. I walked to the corner store, still fuming. *Why in the world he couldn't go get them is beyond me, I thought.*

I decided to take the shortcut through the alley to save time and a few steps. I spoke to my nice but nosy neighbor as I passed. "Hey, Ms. Casey." Her hearing was fading, and whenever she was sitting in the back, I'd always throw my hand up to make sure she saw my friendly wave. She was an older, kind, and gentle lady who sought refuge in her award-winning landscape when the weather was nice enough to sit outside. She always smiled. Sometimes engaging you in small talk.

On my way back, she yelled, "Tell your mother I said hello."

I shouted, "Ok, Ms. Casey, will do." I walked slowly by my garage staring at this black car horizontally parked, blocking my entry. I questioned the audacity and then figured it probably belonged to someone visiting my dad. I squeezed by through the gate and went into the house. "Daddy, I put your tickets on the table."

He walked out of the room and asked, "Did you see it?"

"See what?" By this time, everyone was in the kitchen staring at me. Bub, Denice, Darice, even Ma stopped stirring her pot for a minute or two.

"Your new car!"

"Huh? My new car?" I asked.

"Yea, that's your new convertible parked by the garage." We all ran out the back door. Except Ma, she wasn't running anywhere. We never talked about me getting a car.

"This for me?" He threw me the keys. "Ma?" I said, looking confused.

"Yea, your father picked it out."

Everyone was ecstatic! We got inside, and daddy showed me how to let the top down. Darice hopped in the passenger seat, and Bub and Denice climbed into the back. We blasted the radio and drove down Winchester with onlookers admiring our dopeness. My family planned this unbelievable graduation gift for me, and here I was complaining about getting my dad's lottery tickets. I was a brat who sucked in the worse way. I didn't deserve my parents. I truly didn't.

I jumped back into the dance and modeling circuit. Surprisingly, my modeling gigs increased. In addition to modeling with Fashion Chicago, I was referred to a fashion show producer named Dorothy. She paid well and booked me for many fashion shows, mainly bridal shows. I was even cast in a television commercial modeling furs. Dorothy loved my look. She described it as "exotic." I am not exotic, but Dorothy is white and doesn't know any better.

I never became complacent at the bank and continued to check the career resource center. It was my usual perusing. First, I looked under television, then film, followed by miscellaneous entertainment gigs and dance companies and auditions. Skimming the board, I saw something rather promising. It read, "Part-time work assisting audience, producers, and overall production for a television show." I jotted notes in my notebook and wondered what television show they were referring to. My heart began to beat faster. Maybe this was a positive sign.

The very next day, I called the number listed. I was scheduled for an interview immediately and rushed to the kitchen to tell Ma.

"I have an interview scheduled."

"Who is your interview with?"

"It's for a television show, but I'm not sure which one."

"That's really good. Your perseverance is paying off." She continued cooking.

"The operator mentioned something about Harpo."

"You'll do fine."

I went to the interview and pulled to the front of the building and parked. The first thing I noticed was the pretty colors on the huge marquee. Turquoise and purple cascaded in an obtuse triangle that read "The Oprah Winfrey Show." Flabbergasted, I stared at the wording with the mesmerizing colors for at least two minutes. I simply did not make the connection. Harpo is Oprah spelled backward, duh! Everyone in the world knew that! I sat in my parked car and continued to review my well-rehearsed notes. I took a deep breath and exited my vehicle. The thick glass window separated the employee from the outside. It was an older-looking lady with slightly graying hair cut in a page-boy bob. She sounded like somebody's grandmother. Extremely nice and polite.

"Hello, may I help you?"

"Hi, I have an appointment with Mr. Graves. I'm Patrice Kuykendal."

"Are you here for an interview?"

"Yes, I am." She slid a parking permit under the glass.

"Place this in your window and return it when you leave. Hate for you to get a ticket."

I did what I was told and quickly returned.

"Do you have your ID?" I slid her my ID through the opening. I stood in the vestibule while she ran my name through her computer system. "You are cleared, young lady." She buzzed the glass door and allowed me to enter. She came from behind her desk and handed me my ID back. "Bob will be out shortly. You may go upstairs and have a seat."

I smiled, remembering every person you come in contact with is also interviewing you. "Thank you." The colors in the foyer were warm and welcoming. Shades of earth tones in exquisite marble made up the enormous staircase. It was gorgeous. I took a seat and crossed my ankles. In less than a few minutes, a middle-aged man with hereditary baldness entered. He held the door open and ushered me in. I'll never forget that day or that interview.

It was a paranormal experience. As the Director of Security, Bob was the consummate professional. Ironically, he too, was a fighting leatherneck and also attended Western University back in the day. Which I think was the reason I got my first television job working at The Oprah Winfrey Show.

All of my life, I was told I was a lucky individual. Starting around the age of ten, when my aunt noticed a couple of strands of gray hairs on my head. Distinctively, I can hear her saying, "You know gray hair means you're lucky." It sounded good, so I chose to believe her words.

I almost got a speeding ticket as I rushed home to share the fantastic news. Busting through the front door, I yelled, "Ma!" She is always the first person I look for when sharing good news. Daddy was the only one home. He was in the front room watching the Cowboys play the Steelers, and his favorite player, Tony Dorsett, was dominating. Dallas was by far his beloved team and TD his favorite player. I interrupted. "Daddy, where's Ma?"

Perturbed, he looked up. "I don't know. Gone to the store, perhaps."

I quizzed him. "Daddy, do you know that Harpo is Oprah spelled backward?" He smiled a fake smile. As if to say, you're really disturbing my moment with trivia about The Oprah Show.

"I had an interview there today, and I got the job!"

He perked up with interest. "Oh, yea?"

"I have to give the bank a two-week notice, and then I start."

Daddy's proud facial expression said it all. He smiled. "That's really good," and went back to watching his quarterback murder their opponents.

THE DESTINY

Chapter XV – You Got This

It was unbelievably satisfying to finally break through and get a job in television. My coworkers at the bank were so proud of my accomplishments, and everyone put in their bid for free tickets. My hard work paid off. I didn't quit or give up. I kept checking the career board, waiting, praying for the right opportunity. I started as a Page at The Oprah Winfrey Show. It is basically a runner, an usher, a babysitter, a secretary, or a combination on any given day. I took my position seriously and was eventually promoted to head page to oversee all the others. There's a level of humility in being a page. Yes, it's demeaning. Yes, it's rewarding, but with an industrious work ethic, when you start at the bottom, the only place you can go is up. I wanted my productivity to impress my supervisor for more challenging responsibilities. Most of the pages were young like me, fresh out of college, trying to get their footing in some type of career. The position of a page wasn't sexy or glamourous. It's considered a bottom feeder, and I remember a few of my fellow pages having a hard time with the position. For one, it wasn't full-time and offered no benefits. Nonetheless, I stay encouraged, keeping my eye on the prize in hopes of one day being promoted.

You'd think I would finally hang up my dancing shoes after securing employment at the Oprah Show. Nope. I just had to be more strategic in my approach. I would hit auditions whenever I could, before work, after work, and sometimes even on my lunch break. My hustle ultimately landed me an impressive corporate gig contracted for four weeks. I was the lead dancer, and it paid extremely well. My days became even longer, rehearsing in the evenings and performing on the weekends at the Rosemont Convention Center.

I enjoyed my work. Every day was different, and I loved my coworkers, especially the production guys. I never complained, often stayed late, and worked extra projects. My tenacity eventually paid off, and I was soon promoted. My new responsibilities allowed me to work under the first assistant to the executive producer. I guess that made me second assistant to the executive producer. I still yearned for more. I was determined more than ever to challenge and push myself.

Everyone at work knew I was a dancer and was very supportive. I knew of an upcoming audition for a major touring production, but the time conflicted with my work schedule. I was torn about going. I didn't want to jeopardize my good-paying job, so I decided to make an audition tape, showcasing my many styles of dance. I included pointe/ballet, hip hop, and modern.

On the day of the audition, I mentioned it to my colleague and asked if I should attend. "Ron, there's this audition happening today at noon and they're looking for dancers." Ron was the older brother I never had. He was just as driven, and I appreciated his profound insight and clever keenness. Ron was reserved and quiet by nature. Remarkably, he had opened up to me after a few years of working together, and I knew he would give me a direct, candid response.

"Go, P. You should definitely go."

"I want to, but Ron...sometimes, these things can be cattle call with a gazillion girls."

He stopped what he was doing. "Doesn't matter. You should still go."

"It could take all day, hours."

"I'll take care of the work here. You need to go to that audition."

I was thinking of every excuse of why I shouldn't go, while Ron was giving me every reason why I should.

"Ok, I will go, but if it's too crowded, I'm not staying. I have a thousand things to do here."

"We'll be fine. Don't worry about the office. I'll handle it."

"Thanks!" I smiled and hugged him from behind.

He yelled for me to get off him and reminded me, "You got this P. You got this!" Every girl needs a Ron in their life.

I grabbed my bag and headed out the door. I calculated my time. Ten minutes to downtown, five to park, and another five to find out where I'm going. I entered the Arie Crown Theater and followed the signs to the audition. I had my dance bag and audition tape in hand. I was nervous because I knew in spite of Ron's advocacy, I didn't want to be away from the office too long. My walk turned into a slight jog. I approached a security guard. "Excuse me, do you know where today's auditions are being held?" She pointed straight ahead. "Thanks!" I walked faster, glancing at my watch. I thought, "Shit, I've already been gone twenty-five minutes." I saw a few artsy-looking people and followed them.

A voice bellowed, "Please move to the left and tighten the line."

Yes, I was getting close. I felt the stress in my body. I turned the corner to find what looked like thirty or so people waiting in a line. "Not bad," I thought. I stood behind a lady holding her headshot in her hand. "Excuse me?" She turned around. I asked, "Is this the line to audition?" She smiled and nodded. I pondered, *"I totally can do this and get back to work around 2:00 pm."* I looked back at my watch. Thinking, *"Damn! Thirty minutes have gone by already".* I tried to do the math, but my mind was too preoccupied. I gave up and tried to calm my nerves with a few deep exhales.

I noticed a gentleman walking back and forth with a clipboard sizing up the talent. He would take a few steps and jot notes down. I assumed he was with the show by the way he presented himself. He wasn't that tall and wore a suit with credentials hanging from his neck. After ten minutes elapsed, I decided to approach him.

"Excuse me. Are you with the show?" He was polite.

"Yes, I am."

"Do you know how quickly the line is moving?"

"Put it like this, I hope you packed a lunch. There are maybe a couple of hundred people ahead of you. You can't see it from here, but the front swings into the other room."

The pit of my stomach dropped. "There's no way I'm staying," I thought to myself. "Oh wow!" I turned on the dramatics and softened my voice.

"Unfortunately, I'm unable to stay. I have an audition tape, though. Is there any way you could pass this along to the director?"

"Yes, but you're sure you can't stay?"

"I wish I could, but I'm sorry, I must leave." Guess this is how Cinderella felt when she, too, had to leave the ball.

"Sure, I'll pass it on."

I checked the time again. I took out my audition tape and carefully placed it in his hands. "Thank you kindly, Sir. You have no idea how much this means to me."

He took my tape and walked away. I figured I had nothing to lose and everything to gain. I prayed he would give it to the director and not toss it in the nearest trash. I quickly ran to my car, headed back to work.

Life resumed as normal, and I didn't think any more about the audition or my tape. Months passed, and honestly, I forgot all about the audition, not knowing if my tape actually made it into the director's hands or not.

I was watching TV in my parent's room when the phone rang. I picked up the receiver. It was a lady with a pleasant soft-spoken voice. "Hello, may I speak with Patrice Kuykendal?"

I said, "This is she." She identified herself as Gayle, assistant to the director with Gallant theatrical production company.

"Patrice, do you remember attending an audition about four months ago? You left an audition tape for the director."

"Yes, I do, at the Arie Crown Theater."

"The director has your audition tape, and he was very intrigued with what he saw. He is looking for one more dancer to join our touring production."

I was utterly in disbelief. "Oh, wow!"

"He hasn't fully decided as he is considering you and three more ladies. I'm calling to see if you're still interested and available?"

"Oh yes, I am!"

"I'm getting ahead of myself. Let me tell you a little about the production. It's a fifty-city musical stage play with singers, dancers, and actors. It's a one-year commitment with full salary, housing, and per diem. If you're chosen, we would need you in California this Saturday to start rehearsals." My head was spinning. Today was Wednesday.

I asked, "Do you mean this Saturday?"

"Yes, this Saturday. I know it doesn't provide for much time, but we're moving fast. I will call you tomorrow to let you know the director's final decision."

"Thank you." I hung up the phone. I sat motionless and tried to process everything. How was this even happening?

Everything began to move in slow motion, or was it really fast? I couldn't tell. All I remember is that my head was spinning on its axle, and I felt dizzy. I went to the kitchen, where Ma was.

"Ma." I was immobile. She could tell something was unsettling by the look on my face. After a minute or two, I finally broke through. I said, "Remember I went on that audition on my lunch downtown?"

"Yeah. You didn't stay because there were too many people."

"Right, I left my audition tape with a guy who was working with the show."

"I remember."

"Well, they just called to see if I was still interested and available." Ma just stared at me.

"They're looking for another dancer to join their production. It's a twelve-month tour."

"What did you say?" One thing you have to understand about my mother. She's supportive but also very practical. I'm sure she was thinking, but you've worked so hard to get where you are now.

"I might have to be in LA on Saturday. They're going to call me back tomorrow to let me know if I got it or not. Ma stopped multitasking.

"This Saturday? Today is Wednesday! What about your job?"

"I would have to just wait and see before I say anything."

"Now, start all over and tell me everything, slowly."

We sat at the kitchen table, not saying a word for the first couple of minutes. I was anxious, hesitant, and petrified all at the same time. I thought, *"What if I have to uproot myself?" I have two days to figure everything out.* Daddy came into the kitchen, grabbing a can of beer out of the refrigerator.

"Sonny?" Ma called.

"Yea."

"I think you're going to need to take a seat for this." Daddy remained standing, unsure of what she was about to share. "Patrice just got a call from an audition, and they may need her in Los Angeles this Saturday." He froze.

"I auditioned four months ago, and I couldn't stay because there were so many people there, so I decided to leave my dance audition tape." I couldn't read Daddy's expression. I didn't know if he was excited for me or scared. "It's a fifty-city musical tour. I would be gone for a solid year. They're supposed to let me know for sure tomorrow." Daddy didn't say much. I admit this was a lot to digest, even for him.

"Ok, let me know what they say." He was home for a short break during his swing shift. He placed the beer back in the frig and headed out the kitchen door. Ma looked at me.

"He doesn't believe it."

"How come?"

"Because he doesn't want to. He's afraid of letting you fly. I'll talk to him when he comes home later tonight."

I couldn't sleep. I tossed and turned all night. Got up at least three times. Went to the kitchen just to hold the refrigerator door open. The light illuminated on my face. I didn't want anything from it. I couldn't eat. I still had to go to work and barely woke up on time.

I decided to only share the news with Ron, my ride-or-die coworker. Honestly, if he hadn't motivated and supported me the way he did, I don't think I would have gone. I'm sure I would have talked myself out of auditioning. My relationship with Ron was rock solid. A confidante and a true friend. I remember our supervisor saying, *"Ron must really like you because he doesn't engage with many people."* She was correct. Everyone at work knew Ron as this serious-minded individual. A hard worker, yet very, very reserved.

I got to know and appreciate an entirely different person. Ron was ambitious and grounded and hella funny. In the office, I would always intercept the countless women who called looking for him. He was a female magnet. I recalled when Ron asked my opinion on his decision to propose to his girlfriend at the time.

"P, I'm thinking about doing it."

Clueless, I asked, "About doing what?"

"I'm going to ask Abby to marry me."

I was completely stunned. I stopped what I was doing to sit down. Don't get me wrong, I believe in the union of marriage; I just wasn't sure that Ron did. This was the same guy, who would have at least three different women calling him at work. And as much as I loved Ron, I needed him to be fully prepared both emotionally and physically for such a serious commitment. "Are you sure you're ready? What about Lisa, Yolanda, and Gina? You do know you're gonna have to cut them loose like for real, for real. Plus, all the others lurking in the shadows that I know nothing about. No bullshit Ron McKinney." He knew I was completely serious because I seldomly called him by his government name.

"Just because you say, 'I do,' doesn't mean fairy dust is going to magically sprinkle down, making you an honest, faithful man."

He laughed. "Yeah, I know."

"I'm being serious, Ron. Do you love Abby?"

"You know I do."

"No, I don't. I know on some days, you like her more than the others, but I'm asking if you truly love her?"

He paused before answering and finally said, "Yes, I love her."

"Great, now tell all the others to get lost, or I will next time they call. Abby doesn't deserve that."

"You're right, P. I'll let them know."

Abby was sweet and was by far my favorite. I was rooting for them to win. I secretly prayed Ron would do right by her, and when the time came, he would honor the commitment of his vows.

Ron asked, "You're gonna take it, right?"

"Well, I'm waiting on the final call. Supposed to find out today.

He asked again, "Are. You. Gonna. Say. Yes. To. The. Tour?"

I avoided answering directly. I grew more anxious in my thoughts. The weight of trying to process the last twenty-four hours was a behemoth. I snapped back to reality. "Yes, I think so. I'm talking it over with my parents. I don't have much information, but I'm leaning towards saying yes."

"Isn't this what you've worked for? It's cool working here, and we get our perks, but this was your dream. Now it's finally coming to fruition. P, remember what I said when you left for the audition?"

"Of course, I don't."

"I reminded you of your superpowers, and said, P, you got this!"

It's nice to have people in your corner who believe in you, sometimes more than you believe in yourself. I rushed home and waited for the phone to ring, saying to myself, "Yea, I got this!!!!"

I ran into the house yelling, "Ma!"

Before I could finish my sentence, "No, no one has called yet."

"Oh, ok," I said, trying not to sound too disappointed. "Are you sure? You check the answering machine?"

"There's nothing on the machine."

"Where's daddy?"

"Work."

"Did you get a chance to talk to him about... I mean, you know, if I get it?"

"Your father isn't ready for you to leave home."

"What do you mean?"

"I think he's not accepting that, one, you're a young woman, and two, you may actually leave us in two days, for an entire year. Maybe he's thinking the call was a hoax, a prank, or something else because he doesn't think it could happen. I want you to talk to him. He'll be home in a few hours."

"Ok." I left the room feeling numb. I tried to block out everything, but I couldn't. Even though we had call-waiting, I scolded anyone who got on the phone, and as usual, they paid me no attention.

"Ma! Tell Darice to get off the phone!"

Darice snapped back, "Stupid, we got call waiting!"

"Don't y'all start, please."

Darice yelled from the other room. "That's her, Ma!"

"Ma, sometimes she doesn't click over to answer it."

"Darice, please make sure you answer the other line. She's expecting an important call."

Instead of imploding from her antagonizing, I just went back to the kitchen to put my mind on other things.

Darice came in, looked at me, and said, "Ughhhh!"

I echoed her sentiments, "Ughhhh, back at you." At least I knew she was now off the phone.

The phone rang! I looked at Ma. Darice and I both ran for the phone. Like a linebacker, she pushed me out of the way to grab it first. "Hello, Kuykendal residence. Just a moment. Patrice, telephone," she said while snickering.

I thought, *"God, why couldn't you have given me an older brother instead."* She got on my reserve nerve! I went to my parent's room for some privacy. I closed the door, picked up the receiver, and mellowed my voice.

"Hello, this is Patrice."

"Hi, Patrice. This is Gayle from Gallant's Entertainment. We spoke briefly the other day."

"Yes, I remember."

"Well, Patrice, the director definitely liked your audition tape, and he'd like to cast you as a dancer for this tour. Are you still interested?"

My heart literally jumped out of my body. "YES! Oh, wow. I'm so excited, I don't know what to say?"

"Say you'll take it. We've been auditioning all across the country, and your audition tape impressed him the most. He'll be glad to know that you will be joining the cast. I know this doesn't give you much time, but you have to be in LA this Saturday to start rehearsals. Are you writing all this down?"

"Yes." I quickly grabbed the nearest pen and piece of paper.

"Good. Once you arrive at LAX, a gentleman by the name of Xavier will be holding a sign with your name on it. He will drive you to the hotel, where you will meet your roommate and the rest of the cast. There will be one month of rehearsing before we hit the road. Our first show will open in San Diego. You'll receive a weekly per diem of $350 plus a $750 weekly salary. All room and board will be covered. Patrice, when you pack, anticipate being gone for twelve months, a calendar year, but don't pack too much."

I was trying to capture everything in my notes. It was so much, so fast.

Gayle said, "Take my personal phone number if you have any questions. It's 213-723-7890. I know it is a lot, Patrice. But we are so thrilled you'll be joining us."

I don't remember saying bye or thank you. Afterward, it felt like I floated to the kitchen.

Ma stood there grinning. "I heard, you got it!"

I screamed, "Yes! They want me in LA on Saturday."

"Oh Lord, your dad is gonna lose his mind."

In less than twenty-four hours, my life was turned upside down. I didn't know how or what to pack. I was going to live out of a suitcase for the next twelve months. I was scared. I heard Dad's key turn the lock. Ma must have called and told him, because he headed straight to my room. He sat on the edge of my bed while I pulled clothes out of my dresser. I intentionally avoided eye contact. I didn't want the water well to start. At least not yet. I also didn't want my fear exposed to show him that I was afraid of this new adventure. There was a moment of awkward silence. I kept packing.

Finally, he said, "I don't want you to go, but I know you have to follow your dreams."

And as much as I tried to prevent it from happening, the tears started streaming down my face. I didn't say a word.

"You're gonna be fine," he said. "Just know, I'm so proud of you." He wiped my face, and I tried to swallow the frog that was stuck in my throat.

"Do you know where y'all will perform first?"

I managed to say, "San Diego."

"When you get your schedule, send me a copy. You know the Kuykendals are gonna be front and center in the audience. And if you perform in Memphis, I'll drive down to bring Momma to see you."

As he got up to make his way to the door, I asked, "You'll really bring Grandma?"

He smiled. "Of course, I will."

On Saturday morning, Daddy drove me to the airport. He didn't say much as he walked me to the gate. I hugged him and waved goodbye as I boarded the flight. I didn't turn to look back. I was too emotional already, and I was too scared to be brave. So, I faked it. I found my seat and took a deep breath. As the plane prepared for takeoff, I buckled myself in and thought of Ron's words. *Yes, I really do got this*. I gazed out the window headed to the city of dreams. LA, ready or not, here I come. The End

ABOUT THE AUTHOR

Paula Leland began her career working in television at The Oprah Winfrey Show. She has been a dancer, choreographer, model, teacher, and counselor. As a choreographer and dancer, she toured all over the country with the late comedian Bernie Mac including, performing in his Midnight Mac HBO Comedy special. Additionally, she has performed with artists such as Avant, Queen Latifah, Brian McKnight, and many others.

As a dancer, her art has allowed her to work in Television, Film, and on Broadway, affording her the opportunity to perform across the country. She loves all things fitness and has discovered that returning to her passion of taking dance classes brings her so much joy. A Chicago native, she adores rooting for the Chicago Bears & the Bulls. As an author, she welcomes the role of change agent in hopes to further the inclusion and equity conversations. She believes that you have to see it before you can become it and hopes her book will inspire anyone doubting themselves to pursue their goals. It is her desire that this story will resonate with young adults struggling to find their purpose and place in the world.

When Paula is not writing, she loves spending time with her family, getting lost in a great book and being of service with her beloved sorority. She is ecstatic to share her debut novel, Just let her Dance, from the South Side to Broadway. One girl's Journey into the World of Dance.

To keep in touch with Paula

https://www.LelandPublishing.Media

https://www.Facebook.com/Leland@LelandPublishing.Media

https://www.twitter.com/LelandPublish